VETERAN CARS

F. Wilson McComb

VETERAN CARS

the formative years of motoring

Hamlyn

London · New York · Sydney · Toronto

Acknowledgments The publishers are grateful to the following for the illustrations reproduced in this book:
Associated Press; *Autocar*; British Petroleum; Daimler-Benz; l'Editrice dell'Automobile; Fiat; Ford Motor Company; the Henry Ford Museum; General Motors; David Hodges; Arne Magnussen; F. Wilson McComb; the Mansell Collection; Bill Mason; *Motor*; Musée Française de l'Automobile Henri Malartre; Museo dell'Automobile Carlo Biscaretti di Rufia; the National Motor Museum; Peugeot; Cyril Posthumus; Renault; Rolls-Royce; The Royal Automobile Club; The Science Museum; Standard Register; University of Kansas, Pennell Collection; Veteran Car Club of Great Britain; H. Roger Viollet; David Burgess Wise.

Published by the Hamlyn Publishing Group Limited, London · New York · Sydney · Toronto
Astronaut House, Feltham, Middlesex, England.
Copyright © The Hamlyn Publishing Group Limited, 1974
ISBN 0 600 39130 2

Printed in Czechoslovakia

CONTENTS

THE FORMATIVE YEARS

The motor-car comes in for much abuse these days—especially from the more vociferous sociologists and politicians—as the root of all evil in modern life: overcrowding, pollution, and the ruin of the countryside. Certainly our widespread adoption of this means of transport has brought problems in its wake, but it seems hardly logical to attach so much blame to an inanimate object. If there are too many cars, it can only be because there are too many people. The horse, in its day, was responsible for a level of pollution in our towns that would now be thought intolerable. And the 'unspoiled' countryside, whose passing the sentimentalists so deplore, was a place of back-breaking toil and

appalling poverty for the vast majority who lived in it. The true country dweller, being a realist, welcomes the changes that the internal combustion engine has made in his way of life. He knows that more than any other single invention the motor-car has opened up our lines of communication, helped to dispel ignorance, and brought a higher standard of living to the ordinary man.

In this book I have tried to present a broad picture of the way the motor-car has developed, and something of its impact on our lives, during its earliest and most significant period. There is scarcely any important feature of modern car design that was not already known before the outbreak of the First World War. By that time all the spade-work had been done, and the typical car of 1915 differed far more from its predecessor of 1895 than it does from those we drive today. These two decades, and the one that came before them, were the years that really mattered.

It is customary in Britain to divide early cars into Veteran (up to and including 1904) and Edwardian (1905 to 1918). Other countries have adopted different divisions, and in any case all such classifications are arbitrary ones. I have chosen to follow that laid down by the late Laurence Pomeroy, a gifted motoring writer and son of a gifted designer, because I feel that his summing-up of the crucial 30-year period has never been bettered: 'From 1885 to 1895 men struggled to make the car go. From 1896 to 1905 they contrived to make it go properly. Between 1906 and 1915 they succeeded in making it go beautifully.'

F. Wilson McComb

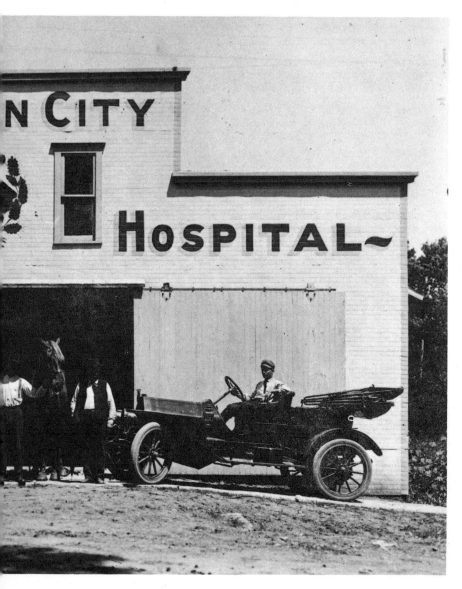

GETTING SOMEPLACE ELSE

Everybody wants to be someplace he ain't. As soon as he gets there he wants to go right back. [Henry Ford, about 1907.]

You only have to look at the human body to see that, whatever purpose it was designed for, it certainly was not high-speed locomotion. As a mechanism for fast movement over the ground, man is a pretty inefficient device compared with, say, any member of the cat family; from this point of view he sacrificed a great deal when, a few million years ago, he decided to get up on his hind legs and move around that way.

This could have been very frustrating when he developed an inquiring mind, a greater urge than any other beast to explore and investigate. But fortunately the erect posture allowed his forefeet to develop into highly sensitive instruments capable of grasping tools and using them. This unique attribute of *homo sapiens,* the combination of hand and brain, enabled him to solve his transport problems, to visit every corner of the globe, and even to move outside it. The astonishing thing is that in the whole span of man's existence the greatest progress has been made in the past 90 years, little more than one lifetime.

If you want to go somewhere without walking, you have to get somebody or something to carry you. The Eastern potentate had his slave-borne litter, the Jacobean nobleman his sedan chair, and you don't need to be rich to find yourself on a hospital stretcher. But speed and distance are limited by human endurance. A man can go farther and faster by climbing onto the back of a suitable quadruped—camel, horse, or what you will.

This discovery is traditionally credited to King Melizyus of Thessaly 'in the golden age of Saturn', whenever that may have been. Certainly it was some thousands of years ago that man started using the horse as a beast of burden, rather than the main course of his evening meal. Until just the day before yesterday, it remained the primary form of transportation on land. It has been developed into many specialised breeds to draw a plough, to carry a knight in armour, to go four-in-hand before a stagecoach, to race and to jump. But somehow the horse has never really got the message. Every single animal still has to be broken in and patiently trained to do its job. Moreover, it has to be shod, groomed and fed—fed every day, as much as three men, whether it is working or not. It is like an engine that must be kept running all the time, with a prodigious fuel consumption even when it is merely idling.

Horses, mules, oxen and even dogs have all been used as draught animals, pulling some kind of conveyance. In its earliest form this was virtually a sledge, a platform mounted on runners. Variants of this, similar to the ultra-simple 'slide car' of the Irish peat bogs, could be seen quite recently in primitive communities as far apart as Scandinavia and Siberia, and as late as 1837 it was reported that there was 'no wheel car' in a Donegal parish of 8000 inhabitants.

It may be that logs were sometimes rolled under these elementary platforms when pulling a particularly heavy load. This would have

'A horse in most harnesses does the work for which his driver is paid; and when the man is more than usual drunk the beast will steer him home. Not so the car. She demands of her driver a certain standard of education, the capacity of unflickering attention and absolute sobriety.'

Rudyard Kipling, 1904

'Go anywhere in England where there are natural, wholesome, contented and really nice English people; and what do you always find? That the stables are the real centre of the household.'

George Bernard Shaw, 1919

Standing room only in a typical Roman chariot, the fastest vehicle of its day.

pointed the way towards the solid disc wheel and thence to the primitive ox-cart, which has scarcely changed at all over the centuries. Then came a much more exciting vehicle, the fighting chariot used by the Hyksos, the 'shepherd kings' of the East, when they invaded Egypt about 1700 BC, and subsequently taken up by the Greeks, the Romans and the ancient Britons. The typical chariot had a light body of wood, wickerwork or leather, fixed directly to the axle, which carried spoked wooden wheels, and a pole ran forward from the axle with a horse yoked to each side of it. With such a power-weight ratio this was obviously a real little sports model, fast and far from comfortable. The warrior and his charioteer stood upright in the bodywork, which was open at the back to allow a rapid exit. When the Romans came to Briton they found the local chariots open at the front, so that the occupants could sit down. This was one of the few British ideas the conquerors considered worth taking back to Rome with them, and before long they had a whole range of special carriages for passenger transport and delivering despatches. Having also built excellent roads, they could really make use of their carriages, and long-distance travel by wheeled vehicle became a reality at last. Some of the later versions had the body hung by leather straps from the rudimentary chassis; it was literally suspended, and to this day we refer to the 'suspension' of a vehicle.

All this progress unfortunately came to an end when the Roman Empire collapsed. The Goths, Vandals and Huns were bonny fighters, but they showed little interest in road-repairing, and for a thousand years and more the highways were neglected. The traveller once again found himself astride a horse, while those who were too sick or too lazy to ride had to make do with the horse litter, a sort of hammock slung between two of the beasts.

With the first stirrings of the Renaissance, carriages began to reappear. By the late 13th century they could be seen in some of the more affluent European capitals, and gradually their numbers increased over the next couple of centuries. But development was slow, very slow. New designs came mostly from the Netherlands, from the Hungarian town of Kocs (which gave us the word 'coach'), and later from England. Samuel Pepys recorded a major advance when, in 1665, he wrote: 'After dinner comes Colonell Blunt, in his new carriage made with springs, as that was of wicker, wherein awhile since we rode at his house. And he hath rode, he says, now this journey, many miles in it with one horse, and outdrives any coach, and outgoes any horse, and so easy, he says. So, for curiosity, I went into it to try it, and up the hill [Shooters Hill] to the heath [Blackheath, London], and over the cart-ruts, and found it pretty well, but not so easy as he pretends.'

It seems incredible that passenger vehicles were known for thousands of years before anyone thought of providing them with proper springs.

'Going through Smithfield I did see a coach run over a coachman's neck and stand upon it, and yet the man rose up and was well after it, which I thought a wonder.'

The Diary of Samuel Pepys, April 8, 1669

Alken, in 1828, foretold chaos and confusion in Regent's Park if steam-driven carriages became all the rage

One possible reason for the slow development of carriages lay in a remarkably widespread bias against them that had persisted since Roman times, at least. It was thought weak, unmanly and decadent to ride in such contraptions, and successive authorities tried to restrict their use by legislation. Roman emperors, a 15th century Pope, one European king after another—all had a go at the unfortunate carriage. The modern motorist, sneaking warily past radar traps and parking meters, may as well be philosophical about his lot; he is up against a prejudice that has existed a long time.

Effective springs were certainly needed, though. Compared with the firm foundations of a Roman road, an occasional shovelful of gravel was a poor substitute, as one Elizabethan writer pointed out: 'When a greate rayne or water commeth, and synketh thorowe the grauell, and commeth to the earthe, then the earthe swalleth and bolneth and waxeth softe, and with treadynge, and specially with caryage, the grauell synketh, and goeth downward as his natures kynd requyreth, and then it is in a

maner of a quycke sande, that hard it is for anything to goo over.'
Henry VIII had required landowners to keep the roads in repair, and
Mary, half-a-century later, had called on the inhabitants of every parish
to devote four days a year to roadwork. But both these attempts failed,
and there was little improvement when the first English turnpikes were
set up to finance roadbuilding and repair from the proceeds of toll
charges, although 22 000 miles of road were laid or maintained under
this system.

By the late 18th century those who could afford it were able to make
quite lengthy, if uncomfortable, journeys on wheels, famous inns were
linked by stagecoach services, and mails were regularly carried. In 1804
Elliot invented the elliptical leaf-spring. Telford (nicknamed 'The
Colossus of Roads') and his fellow-Scot McAdam (whose name lives on
in 'tarmacadam' although this surface was invented in 1907, some 70
years after his death) brought scientific methods to bear on roadwork.
With better roads, carriages became lighter and more refined in
construction, vastly different from the lumbering farm-wagon.

Even so, travel by road was such a slow and expensive business that,
as the historian E.J. Hobsbawn has commented, it was easier to reach
another country by sea than to travel overland in one's own: London
was closer to Plymouth, or even to Edinburgh, than to the inland villages
of Norfolk. An earlier historian, Edward Gibbon, went by coach across
Europe in 1793 when he travelled from Lausanne to Ostend, following
an indirect route to avoid the dangers of the French Revolution. His
650-mile journey, starting soon after sunrise every day, occupied a full
three weeks.

Ironically enough it was Gibbon himself who had recorded how one
Caesarius covered an almost identical distance by chariot, from Antioch
to Constantinople, in only six days – and that was in the 4th century.
Until the early 1800s, no man could travel any faster on land than the
Romans had done some 1 500 years before, and the only way to speed
things up was to find something to replace the horse.

*Two popular types of horse-drawn
vehicle, the game cart* (top right)
and the station wagon (right),
*strongly influenced the shape of the
horseless carriages that followed.*

THE MOVING FORCE

Soon shall thy arm, unconquered steam, afar
Drag the slow barge, or drive the rapid car
Erasmus Darwin, 1792.
. . . that divelish yron engin, wrought in deepest hell
Edmund Spenser, about 1589.

One alternative to the horse that attracted surprisingly much attention
over the centuries was self-propulsion, in one form or another. As far
back as the 8th century the Chinese are said to have propelled wheeled
vehicles over the land by means of oars, which, if nothing else, is one
way to avoid being seasick. In 1649 Johann Hautsch of Nuremberg
built a splendidly-decorated carriage described as 'going by spring'
(though some said it was operated by sweating minions concealed in the
interior). But if it went at all it did so in a straight line, for the inventor
omitted to provide a steering mechanism. At the tender age of 13 the
great Isaac Newton built a four-wheeler that could be moved by rotating
a handle – a kind of invalid carriage, in fact – and somewhat similar
devices were built at intervals throughout the 18th century. Another
noted English scientist, Robert Hooke, patented a peculiar means of
transport in 1664. Hooke had the reputation of being 'irritable,
penurious and solitary', and for a combination of economy and
misanthropy he certainly excelled himself by providing only one wheel
with the rider *inside* it. However, Dr Hooke also invented the universal
joint, without which our cars might still be driven by belts and pulleys.

The early 19th century brought the hobbyhorse, a simple two-
wheeled framework 'paddled' along with the feet, which earned the
name of dandyhorse by becoming a plaything of the idle rich. A Scottish
engineer, MacMillan, introduced a more practical note in 1839 by
providing one of them with oscillating cranks and stirrups, and some 20
years later the Michaux brothers of Paris took the next important step

*The Dutch sail wagon was one of the
odder experiments in horseless
propulsion. This one was built for
Prince Maurice of Nassau in 1600
by his tutor, Simon Stevin.*

forward by fitting rotary cranks to their 'boneshakers'. Soon after this, the desire for more speed brought Starley's 'penny farthing' or 'ordinary' bicycle with its enormous front wheel, and in 1874 H.J. Lawson finally set the pattern by inventing the 'safety bicycle', the first to have chain drive and equal-diameter wheels. With the arrival of Dunlop's pneumatic tyre in 1888, the bicycle attained widespread popularity, and it was to have two profound influences on the development of the motor-car. On the one hand it taught manufacturers how to achieve strength without excessive weight, which was a novel idea in those days. On the other, it enabled people, rich or poor, to enjoy for the first time the unique pleasures of *individual* transportation. With little effort and in complete freedom, they were at last able to explore the countryside around them.

But the motor-car needs a motor, and for a very long time nobody could agree what form this should take. In the 17th century, the Dutch experimented with sail wagons, and in America it was claimed that a clockwork-driven bus ran as late as 1870. One possible source of power was the steam engine, which had been produced in a very primitive form before the birth of Christ. Another was to use the explosive force of gunpowder, first employed in cannon by Genghis Khan in 1234. Many years later it was realised that some other explosive mixture would be better, and this was the first effective step towards 'putting the furnace inside the cylinder', as Professor Andrade expressed it; in other words, to the development of the internal combustion engine. However, the early engines of this type were so crude that at first the smooth-running steam engine seemed a much more promising choice.

The earliest steam engines (apart from the reaction-type 'aeolopile' built in the 2nd century BC by Hero of Alexandria) were usually intended for pumping water, and the steam was merely condensed inside a container to cause a vacuum—atmospheric pressure did the work. The engine suggested by Battista della Porta in 1601 was of this type, something similar was described by the Marquis of Worcester in 1663, and the design patented by Savory in 1698—the first practical steam engine used in industry—still followed the atmospheric principle. Meanwhile the Dutch physicist, Huygens, had proposed a gunpowder engine. His assistant, Denis Papin, seemed unable to decide between gunpowder and steam, but he did favour the use of a piston, which Newcomen adopted for his steam engine of 1705. Then came that well-known figure, James Watt, who made several notable improvements to Newcomen's engine between 1761 and 1781.

A piston moves in a straight line, and for most purposes this movement has to be converted into a rotary one so that the power of the engine can be utilised. Watt was unable to use the obvious mechanism – a crank and connecting rod – because of a patent held by his contemporary, James Pickard, and had to resort to a most unwieldly

'I think the most ridiculous sight in the world is a man on a bicycle, working away with his feet as hard as he possibly can, and believing that his horse is carrying him, instead of, as anyone can see, he carrying the horse.'

George Bernard Shaw, about 1881

The world's oldest surviving mechanically-propelled vehicle, Cugnot's steam tractor of 1770, may still be seen in a Paris museum today.

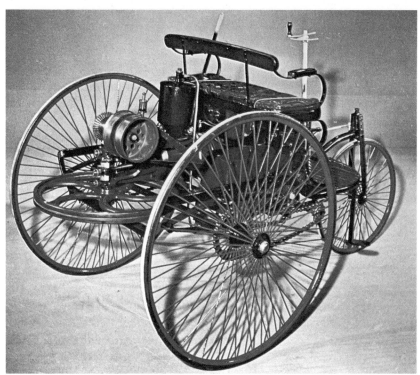

*The first examples of three famous
makes : Henry Ford's original
experimental car of 1896 (left);
the Benz three-wheeler of 1885
(top); Daimler's first four-wheeler,
a horse-drawn carriage fitted with
an engine in 1886 (above).*

arrangement. Throughout the 18th and 19th centuries, development was repeatedly held up by such disputes over patents, and Watt himself was capable of being just as dog-in-the-manger over his own inventions.

Meanwhile over in France another engineer, Nicholas Joseph Cugnot, was designing what is generally considered the world's first mechanically-propelled vehicle. One of these was built by Brézin in 1769 for the French government (who wanted it for the transport of cannon), and a larger one, which is still in existence, in 1771. The Cugnot steam carriage has been dismissed as cumbersome and hopelessly inefficient, which it certainly was: it was driven *and* steered by its single front wheel, which was rotated by ratchet and pawl, and carried the whole weight of the machinery. But Cugnot was clever enough to use high pressure steam in his twin-cyclinder engine, and at least his vehicle worked–though it took about an hour to cover one kilometre.

William Murdock, assistant to James Watt, might well have built a successful steam carriage shortly after Cugnot–he made at least one working model in Cornwall in about 1781, and this little device, which was crank-driven, ran very well. However, Watt took exception to these experiments and ensured that Murdock was kept busy with other work. Indeed, he himself took out a patent for a steam carriage in 1784 'to keep other people from similar patents'. Watt did say that he was 'resolved to try if God will work a miracle with these carriages', but even with such an exalted collaborator he seems to have devoted little attention to the project.

These were the great days of the Cornish mining industry which did so much to develop steam power, and one of the leading figures was that under-rated genius, Richard Trevithick. The man who really pioneered the successful application of high-pressure steam (which Watt greatly distrusted), Trevithick built and tested a roadgoing steam carriage in 1801, and another two years later. The second version had a separate crankshaft geared to the driving wheels, and Trevithick anticipated the need to provide a variable-ratio transmission, although 'gear changing' then meant literally changing the gears. Some say that Trevithick's engine designs were copied from those of the American exponent of high-pressure steam, Oliver Evans, who took out a patent for steam wagons in Maryland in 1787. But Evans' nearest approach to actually building one came in 1805, when he used the engine of a steam-driven dock pontoon to propel it the mile-and-a-half from his workshop to the harbour where it was to be employed.

But the internal combustion engine had not been forgotten. We know tantalisingly little about the piston engine described in 1794 by an Englishman named Street, though it used a mixture of air with vapourised turpentine, and has been called the first British gas engine. In 1805 a Swiss, de Rivaz, produced a free-piston hydrogen engine with electric ignition and actually fitted it in a carriage which it drove–more or less–by rack and pinion. Then in 1808 Sir George Cayley, the aeronautical pioneer who insisted on making his experimental aeroplanes bird-shaped, rather oddly put the clock back by building a gunpowder engine for one of them. Some say that Street was the first to use a form of hot-tube ignition, some say it was Cayley, and some give the credit to Daimler, about 80 years later.

In the de Rivaz engine the explosion merely raised a heavy piston, which then fell under its own weight and drove the mechanism in doing so. That is to say, the actual work was done by gravity, rather as in the early steam engines the work was done by atmospheric pressure. Cecil's 1820 hydrogen-air engine had a foot in both camps, being an internal combustion unit used to create a vacuum, like a steam engine, and Samuel Brown's 1824 gas-vacuum engine worked on the same principle. Brown fitted his in a carriage and successfully climbed Shooters' Hill, Blackheath (where another Samuel, Pepys, had tried out the 'new carriage made with springs' 160 years before). Then came a notable

'In my opinion if a person brings on to a highway a machine worked by a series of explosions of an explosive mixture, and from some cause or other directly connected with the working of the machine, an explosion of this mixture does occur accompanied by a noise calculated to frighten a horse of ordinary nerve, courage, temper and training, to such an extent as to endanger the person riding or driving it, the machine is for the time being a nuisance, and the owner responsible for any danger caused thereby.'

Judgment by His Honour Judge Lindley quoted in *The Autocar*, March 12, 1910

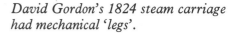
David Gordon's 1824 steam carriage had mechanical 'legs'.

advance with William Barnett's gas engine of 1838, for Barnett realised that more power could be obtained by compressing the charge before ignition – something that the gunpowder enthusiasts, after all, had already known.

By this time, however, the adherents of steam were well ahead where transportation was concerned. Griffiths, Burstall and Hill, James, Gordon, Hancock, Gurney, Dietz in France, Bordano in Italy, Fisher in America and many others had all succeeded in building steam-powered coaches. Several of them, by the early 1830s, had started running regular passenger services on a commercial basis. If some of their ideas were a little peculiar (Gurney and Gordon both thought their coaches should have mechanical legs to help them up hills, and Gibbs and Chaplin arranged for all four wheels to be steered), they were making the first effective approaches towards solving the problems of steering, suspension and transmission in a mechanically-propelled vehicle. Unfortunately they encountered prejudice and opposition on almost every side: from farm labourers, who made violent attacks on them with cries of 'Down with all machinery!'; from those with vested interests in the fast-developing railways, who wanted all 'locomotives' to run on rails; from those in charge of turnpikes, who imposed on the steam carriages tolls that were anything up to 12 times the charges made

Dr Church's ponderous and highly decorated 1833 steamer carried 50 passengers between London and Birmingham.

for a four-horse coach (although Telford himself said that steam carriages did less damage to the roads). In the early 1860s a uniform scale of tolls was laid down, but it was accompanied in 1865 by an Act of Parliament that almost killed the development of all horseless carriages in Britain by imposing a 4 mph speed limit (2 mph in towns) and requiring three attendants, one walking 60 yards ahead with a red flag, to every vehicle. American pioneers met similar opposition: their flagman had to walk 100 yards ahead, steam automobiles had to be approved by the appropriate city department, and their operators were expected to have an engineer's licence (which required several years' apprenticeship as a fireman!).

So the initiative passed back to the Continent of Europe, where several important advances in engine design had already been made. In 1859, Barsanti and Matteucci produced an internal combustion engine which, like that of de Rivaz half-a-century before, was a free-piston design. In 1860 a Belgian, Lenoir, built what was virtually a double-acting steam engine adapted to work as a two-stroke gas engine, with electric ignition. Using uncompressed gas, it had a heavy fuel consumption but ran reliably at around 100 rpm, and was successfully marketed; Lenoir even built a car of sorts, though its speed worked out at a modest 2 mph. Then, in 1862, Beau de Rochas of Paris laid down the principles of the four-stroke internal combustion engine—the basic design that is used to this day.

At the Paris Exhibition five years later, Otto and Langen of Karlsruhe showed their version of the free-piston engine. This 'mechanical outrage', as G. A. Burls has called it, needed a cylinder 13 feet high to produce 3 horsepower, and in the words of Anthony Bird, made a noise like a brontosaurus with hiccups. It was a far from efficient device, but it

Crankshaft, big end and drive gears of the 1885 Benz tricycle were all exposed to road dust and dirt. The engine was started by pulling the flywheel.

superseded the Lenoir engine on the market because it used less than half as much fuel, and in 1877 the same company followed it with their famous 'silent gas engine' working on the four-stroke principle. It seems rather unfair that this has since become known as the 'Otto cycle'; the principle had first been proposed by Beau de Rochas and the engine owed much to the work of two of Dr Otto's employees, Gottlieb Daimler and Wilhelm Maybach. Perhaps that is why they left the company in 1882 and set up their own business in Cannstatt, where they continued their experiments. At first, all they succeeded in doing was to arouse the suspicions of the local inhabitants, who decided that Mr Daimler and Mr Maybach were making counterfeit coinage and sent a posse to their workshop to unmask the conspirators.

Another ex-Otto employee, Karl Benz, had marketed an internal combustion engine in 1879. Of necessity this was a two-stroke, because of the patent that Otto had secured. This worked well and his business prospered. When the Otto patent was later ruled invalid, Benz brought out a small four-stroke gas engine which ran at about 300 rpm, using electric ignition. About the same time, Daimler and Maybach produced their new four-stroke petrol engine, which ran at the unheard-of speed of 800 rpm. In 1885 a small version of the Daimler engine was fitted to a boneshaker bicycle with two stabiliser wheels, and the following year another was installed in a horse-drawn carriage from which the shafts had been removed. Also in 1885, Benz modified one of his engines for use in a light three-wheeled carriage which he had built on bicycle lines.

Thus Daimler and Benz laid the foundations for the development of the successful petrol-engined car. Daimler, with Maybach, appreciated the need to run an engine at comparatively high speed to obtain sufficient power from a small unit, but the Cannstatt organisation then

Amédée Bollée's 12-seater steam coach of 1873 may have looked peculiar, but it had well-designed steering and independent front suspension.

This 1894 picture of a Benz family outing shows how early motor-cars still resembled the horse-drawn vehicles that preceded them.

turned to other projects for a number of years. Benz, having produced a vehicle that worked, continued its development until it became a commercial proposition.

There were others, of course, who played their parts at this time. The steam enthusiasts had not been idle, and one of them, J.H. Knight of Farnham, had built a steam carriage despite the very restrictive legislation that he faced in England. In 1873 came the first vehicle of that mechanical genius, Amédée Bollée of Le Mans—a 12-seater steam coach with Lankensperger (now known as Ackermann) steering and independent front suspension. Bollée built many more successful steam vehicles, tried less successfully to market them, and—perhaps most important—aroused the enthusiasm of two of his sons, who were soon to make their impact upon the motoring world.

In Paris, in 1881, the elegant and aristocratic Comte de Dion met two builders of model steam engines, Bouton and Trépardoux, and persuaded them to join him in an enterprise that was to have a far-reaching effect upon the development of the motor-car.

From oars and levers, sails and clockwork, the horseless carriage had come a long way. Power units—steam or petrol—had been made small enough to install in a fairly light conveyance and still leave room for some passengers, so that powered vehicles became more than mere boilers-on-wheels, became worth considering as a possible means of private and personal transportation instead of being omnibuses, like the steam coaches of half-a-century before. But as yet they were little more than a possibility, the obsession of a few eccentric individuals, and most people relied on the fast-developing railway system when they wanted to travel any distance overland. For shorter journeys, they still climbed on a horse.

MAKING IT GO

The purchaser must not expect too much from his motor carriage. Sir David Salomons advises purchasers to see the machine taken to pieces, and put together. This may possibly take up a whole day, or even more, but it is time well spent and will save many a disappointment afterwards. It is absolutely necessary that those who have charge of motor carriages should understand the machinery they look after. Breakdowns will occur, causing vexatious delays, but by careful management they often may be avoided.
J.H. Knight, *Notes on Motor Carriages,* 1896.

Having transformed the horseless carriage from a dream into a reality, man faced a whole host of new problems whose very existence he had not suspected before. When your carriage is drawn by a horse you sit high in the air, partly so that you can see over the brute, and partly for reasons it would be indelicate to dwell upon. The front axle is pivoted at the centre for going around corners, and the front wheels are small so that they may pass underneath the carriage when turning. Your carriage is handier and more manœuvrable if the front and back wheels are fairly close together. As for the springing, this can be as soft as you like without introducing serious complications in other directions.

Take away the horse, and then what? After a time (and it took a surprisingly long time) you start asking *why* you should be perched so far from the ground. You find that without horse and shafts in front, the centre-pivoted axle behaves quite differently and may become uncontrollable when one wheel hits a bump. So you have to adopt some other form of steering—and then, why should the front wheels be smaller? You find, too, that when the horse has been put inside the carriage, so to speak, the wheelbase has to be longer to allow more room for passengers; indeed, your horseless carriage seems to steer better that way. Now that you are travelling faster you really need softer springing, but it is difficult to provide any springing at all when you have a transmission system linked to the wheels.

You can simplify the steering by having just a single wheel at the front, but you have to arrange for each back wheel to rotate at a different speed on corners (a problem you hadn't properly appreciated when all the wheels were merely running free, instead of being driven). One way of dodging the need for a differential gear is to drive just one back wheel, but you soon find this is not a clever idea. Another is to put the single wheel at the back, but then you have the greater complexity of two wheels to steer at the front. It is hard to decide the best place for the engine; indeed, you still haven't decided what type of engine is best: steam, petrol, or even an electric motor. The electric motor needs an enormous bank of heavy batteries to give your carriage even a limited range, but it is very smooth-running. The steam engine is almost as smooth, but with its attendant boiler and burners and whatnot, it too makes a heavy installation. The petrol engine is lighter but vibrates a great deal and does not develop maximum torque until it is running quite fast; further, it is so inflexible that you have to provide different gear ratios.

These, and many more, were the questions the early designers asked themselves, and at first they found many different answers. If some of their solutions seem absurd to us today, we have to remember that they were venturing into unknown territory. The right answer was by no means always obvious. When Gustav Hammel of Denmark built his 1886 car, he had the strange notion that the wheel should be turned to

'A man who has never owned an automobile rather expects it to provide all the delights and abilities of a private railway train, a racing-stable, a coach-and-four, a smart span of horses, a safe family hack, a pony cart for the children, and a morning walk.'

R.T. Sloss, *The Book of the Motor Car,* **1905**

'On the day when a cheap, light, and compact means of storing a great power of electricity is discovered we shall see the last of the motor-car as we know it at present.'

Filson Young, *The Complete Motorist,* **1905**

the left to steer it to the right. But it was then a very novel idea to have a steering wheel at all.

Karl Benz had favoured the single front wheel on his 1885 car, placing the engine horizontally at the rear with belt drive to a countershaft that incorporated a differential gear, and thence by side chains to the rear wheels. It was not an ideal arrangement, but it worked, and he adhered to it for many years. Gradually he improved his original design in detail, increasing the power output and installing a two-speed gear. By 1887 Emile Roger had secured the selling rights in France, where other builders soon began to copy the Benz-style carriages that Roger was assembling there.

Meanwhile a Belgian, Edouard Sarazin, started negotiating for the right to build Daimler engines in France, entrusting their manufacture to Panhard and Levassor, makers of woodworking machinery. When Sarazin died suddenly in 1887 his widow secured the concession, became acquainted with Levassor, and married him in 1890. This romantic occurrence was to have a considerable effect on the developing French motor industry, for by now Daimler had designed a new vee-twin engine capable of 900 rpm and installed it experimentally in a quadricycle with transmission by sliding spur gears and side chains. Panhard-Levassor, their rights to the Daimler engine comfortably established by Mme Sarazin's second marriage, decided to use the new version as the basis of a carriage which they would build themselves.

While Daimler and Benz were developing better internal combustion

Gottlieb Daimler's twin-cylinder engine, marketed early in 1889, gave the car makers a source of much more power with little increase in weight.

The driver of the 1886 Hammel (which still survives) concentrates hard because the wheel turns left to steer it to the right.

engines in Germany, a leading French engineer, Léon Serpollet, was greatly improving the steam engine, and in 1888 produced his new 'flash' boiler. This was seen at the 1889 Paris Exhibition by one of the Peugeot brothers, who had recently added bicycle manufacture to their many other interests. The upshot of this, in 1890, was a rather clumsy three-wheeled steamer which Peugeot and Serpollet managed to coax from Paris to Lyons, some 300 miles. By all accounts the journey was a fairly traumatic experience (Serpollet himself likened it to Nansen's first Arctic expedition of the previous year). It certainly put an end to Peugeot's short-lived enthusiasm for the steam engine, and his company designed a new carriage propelled by the Daimler engine, which they bought from Panhard-Levassor. This first Peugeot petrol car owed much to bicycle-building practice–it even had handlebar steering–and in 1891 achieved the very remarkable feat of covering no less than 1500 miles at an average speed of 10 mph.

The Comte de Dion, with his partners Bouton and Trépardoux, had been building successful steam carriages for several years by this time, and one of their quadricycles had 'won' an event organised by a Paris cycling journal, *Le Vélocipède*, in 1887; it might, perhaps, be called the world's first motoring competition–except that de Dion was the only competitor. However, while Armand Peugeot was studying the Serpollet boiler at the 1889 Exhibition, the worthy Count was taking a much keener interest in the various internal combustion engines that were also on show. He too was becoming disenchanted with steam, and turned to the petrol engine with such enthusiasm that he and Georges Bouton started experimenting with rotary units of four and even 12 cylinders; it was odd, really, that their initial research was in this direction, for they were to become world famous for their single-cylinder engines. Trépardoux, however, was appalled by all this messing about with 'explosion motors', left the firm in disgust, and thus severed his connection with the motor-car factory that soon grew into the biggest in the world. Poor Trépardoux; he really *did* back the wrong horse.

By 1893 things were beginning to look interesting. The Benz had become a four-wheeler with Lankensperger steering controlled by rack-and-pinion. With its engine running at around 600 rpm, it was capable of about 15 mph, it was now definitely a commercial proposition and selling quite steadily, especially in France, where it enjoyed Emile Roger's enthusiastic support. Daimler had formed a company to build cars, although this got off to a poor start when Daimler and Maybach left for a time after a disagreement with the management, and nothing worthwhile was produced until their return. However, the relatively

high-speed Daimler engine, built by Panhard-Levassor, was at least being used by the two leading French car-makers.

In England a Walthamstow enthusiast named Frederick Bremer was working on a crude little rear-engined car, and a far more advanced vehicle was just beginning to take shape in the highly analytical mind of Frederick Lanchester. In faraway America, John Lambert of Ohio and Henry Nadig of Pennsylvania had both succeeded in building cars, and the Duryea brothers were endeavouring to do so in Massachusetts.

Panhard-Levassor, after experimenting with a mid-engined car, had placed their engine in front under a 'box-like structure' which came to be called a bonnet in England or a hood in America. The drive was taken through a friction clutch to a countershaft which provided different gear ratios and a reverse, then by side chains to the rear wheels. The Lankensperger steering was controlled by a tiller, there was a sidebrake operating on the rear wheels, and a footbrake applied to the transmission. This Panhard-Levassor was a lofty and clumsy brute, far from easy to drive, by comparison with the light, elegant and low-slung Peugeot, but its designer had somehow stumbled on the best layout for the major components of a motor-car, the one that almost all other designers eventually copied. As Beau de Rochas was responsible for the 'Otto' four-stroke principle, Lankensperger invented 'Ackermann' steering and Trépardoux designed the 'de Dion' rear axle, it follows that this arrangement, the work of Emile Levassor, became known to all as the *système Panhard*.

At the end of 1893 another French cycling paper, *Le Petit Journal*, caused great excitement by announcing their plans for the world's first motor rally, and entries began to pour in. The 102 application forms showed all too clearly that most hopeful designers of horseless carriages were still living in cloud cuckoo land. The first applicant, a Monsieur Rousselet, chose gravity as his motive power, and several plumped for 'weight of passengers'. Some planned to run on compressed air, some on 'combined liquids' or various arrangements of pedals and levers, and Messieurs Garnier and Delannoy specified 'a combination of animate and mechanical motor'. A mouse in a treadmill, perhaps? We shall never know, for their carriage was not among the 26 that finally appeared after two postponements of the event.

A short eliminating trial brought the total down to 21 for the run of almost 80 miles from Paris to Rouen on July 22 1894. Eight were steamers and 13 petrol-driven, including five Peugeots and four

Panhard-Levassor cars. The competition was dominated by the Comte de Dion's entry, a steam tractor drawing a landau from which the front axle and shafts had been removed, and this odd-looking contrivance was the first to arrive, followed by two Peugeots. But the judges decided that, needing a stoker as well as a driver, it did not meet the requirement of being 'easily handled'. As for the Peugeots, it was pointed out that they used Panhard-Levassor (ie, Daimler) engines, so first prize was jointly awarded to Peugeot and Panhard.

That first prize should go to the machine which did not finish first will surprise nobody who has taken part in a French motor rally. The really significant result was that every single one of the 13 petrol cars completed the run, at speeds varying from 11·5 mph down to 7·9 mph, beating all the steamers except the de Dion tractor, and of the remaining seven steamers only three reached the finish. This did much to encourage designers to take a greater interest in petrol cars.

Indeed, the event aroused interest throughout France, for as one passenger recorded, 'At the windows and doors old people saluted with emotion these vehicles of the future, of the very near future. School-masters and nuns brought their pupils out to be present at a spectacle which will long be remembered in the annals of the country.' Fired with enthusiasm (despite his exclusion from the awards list) the Comte de Dion now suggested a much sterner test–a race, this time, over several hundred miles. Early in November 1894 a score of interested parties met at his house to discuss the idea, and this committee formed the nucleus of the oldest motoring club in existence, the Automobile Club de France. Before the year ended they had published their itinerary for a race all the way from Paris to Bordeaux *and back again*.

It was an almost absurdly ambitious scheme. The driver of today, looking at a typical car of the period with its tiller steering, solid rubber tyres, rudimentary springing and flickering oil-lamps, would think twice about taking it much farther than just around the block. We are highly impressed when meticulously-restored survivors of that era trundle the 53 miles from London to Brighton in broad daylight on smoothly-surfaced roads. What, then, of the world's first motor race–732 miles to be covered flat out, by day and by night, without any outside assistance in the case of a breakdown? How they did it defies comprehension, but the crews of nine of the 22 vehicles that left Versailles on June 11 1895 succeeded in completing the full distance within their allotted time. In

'No man should be allowed to design a car until he has spent at least two years in a general repair shop.'

David J. Smith, *The Autocar*, **January 13, 1912**

Peugeot, having abandoned their experiments with steam, used their experience of bicycle manufacture to design lightweight petrol-engined cars. This elegant vehicle was built for the Bey of Tunis in 1892.

what is surely the greatest motoring achievement ever, Emile Levassor stuck grimly to his Panhard to finish first, 'covered in dust and flowers' (thrown by excited spectators), at an overall average speed of 15 mph. Other competitors shared the driving, but not Levassor, who drove for 48 hours 48 minutes, and stopped for a mere 10 minutes at Bordeaux. It was a superhuman performance. Yet Levassor was not declared the winner; the regulations called for the cars to seat more than two passengers, and his was only a two-seater.

Once again the petrol car proved its supremacy. The competing vehicles were 13 of this type, mostly Peugeot or Panhard, six steamers, one electric car and two motorcycles. Eight petrol cars occupied the first eight places and Amédée Bollée's veteran steam omnibus, built in 1880, was ninth and last. Jeantaud's electric car dropped out in the early stages, although he had spent £1000 on replacement batteries to await him along the route.

The Panhards and Peugeots were fitted with a new 4 hp parallel-twin engine which was basically a Daimler type, but in the main designed by Levassor himself. On the face of it the new Phénix-Daimler engine, as it was called, offered no startling advantage over the earlier vee-twin, but in fact its advent was of considerable importance. Once you have put two cylinders in tandem there is nothing to stop you adding *more* cylinders—which, indeed, Levassor did the following year, thus pointing the way towards the modern in-line multi-cylinder engine.

Two other significant technical developments were associated with the 1895 Paris-Bordeaux race. One Peugeot, driven by André Michelin, was fitted with pneumatic tyres. They gave continual trouble, the unfortunate Michelin mending countless punctures and using up 22 spare tubes before he finally had to drop out, and Levassor commented that pneumatic tyres would obviously never be any use on motor-cars. But Michelin stubbornly persevered with his 'useless' tyres. Another vehicle, which did not start at all because it was not ready in time, was the latest de Dion motor tricycle. Its first appearance in running order, shortly afterwards, represented another major step forward. De Dion and Bouton had produced a light and handy machine with a completely new petrol engine, small in size but running at the fantastic speed of 2000 rpm. When Georges Bouton first built this engine and ran it at 900 rpm (about the speed of the Phénix-Daimler) he encountered continual bearing trouble, and was amazed to find that by doubling its speed he could make it work beautifully, with, of course, a substantial increase in power output. Quite by accident he had discovered that a petrol engine would run better at really high rpm, a notion that was heresy to the gas engine mentality of most other designers. And in doing so he developed the coil ignition system that we use to this day.

These early motoring competitions undoubtedly made the leading car builders of the 1890s more aware of the problems that lay before them, and forced them to adopt a less horse-minded approach to the design of the horseless carriage. In this atmosphere, particularly in France, rapid technical progress was inevitable, while the enthusiasm inseparable from motor racing infected everyone to some extent. By the end of 1894, Peugeot had built and sold almost 80 cars, Panhard 90, and the total production of Benz cars had reached 271.

Karl Benz had certainly got away to a good start as the world's first motor manufacturer, but his rear-engined, belt-driven 'Viktoria', if popular because of its simplicity and reliability, was not at all forward-looking in design. In Germany he lacked the impetus to improve his vehicles that motor racing provides, and before long he had occasion to regret this when sales of his then outmoded cars began to decline. The Cannstatt-Daimler organisation suffered in the same way. By the end of 1895 they at last got a car into production, but with its centre-point steering and no rear suspension at all it was an even more archaic vehicle than the Benz; its only significant feature was a mechanism for

Emile Levassor was the man behind the Phénix-Daimler engine. With one cylinder placed behind the other, this pointed the way towards the modern multi-cylinder unit.

controlling the belt-pulleys that foreshadowed the gate-change gear
lever. Daimler eventually found their salvation in motor racing when
they were persuaded to build a model for that particular purpose.

In America, although there were hardly any roads and only a handful
of experimental car-builders, the *Chicago Times-Herald* optimistically
offered a $5 000 prize for a race to be run on November 2 1895. Only
two cars appeared at the start: a Duryea, which landed in a ditch when
the driver swerved to avoid a horse-drawn wagon, and a Benz which
finished the 92-mile course in solitary glory. The organisers tried again
on Thanksgiving Day with six cars, of which two–the Benz and the
Duryea–completed a shortened course in thick snow, whereupon both
of them were disqualified for some unrecorded reason. Yet another
attempt was made in New York the following May with even worse
results: only one finisher, at not much more than 18 mph. It seemed that
America was not really ready for motor racing.

In England, with its 4 mph speed limit, there could be no question of
holding races; it was almost against the law to use a horseless carriage
on the road at all, and few had the temerity to do so. One of the
exceptions was John Henry Knight, who in 1895 followed up his earlier
steam-powered carriage experiments by building a petrol-engined
tricycle, but after covering a mere 150 miles he was sternly brought to
book and fined half-a-crown for this display of pioneering spirit. The
Hon. Evelyn Ellis, the Hon. Charles Rolls and Sir David Salomons
deliberately flouted authority by importing foreign cars and driving
them, but they were too aristocratic to be fined like the humble Mr
Knight. Another prominent motoring enthusiast, Harry Hewetson, had
a Benz delivered to him late in 1894 (it cost £80 9s 9d) and, a few
months later, decided to give it an airing in London. Setting off from
Liverpool Street station, he got no further than Charing Cross before
he was stopped by the police, who took his name and address and sent
him off to Scotland Yard. There he was magnanimously let off with a

*It was Levassor, too, who averaged
15 mph in the world's first motor
race, all the way from Paris to
Bordeaux and back again, in 1895.
He drove almost non-stop for two
days and nights.*

*Compare this 1898 Panhard with
the 1894 car on page 23 to see how
racing improved the breed in a few
short years. A steering wheel has
replaced the tiller, there is a four-
cylinder engine, clutch and gears are
enclosed, and the equal-sized wheels
are shod with pneumatic tyres.*

caution after being told—like a naughty child in the nursery—that he
must not do it again. In Scotland, T.R.B. Elliott of Kelso bought a
Panhard at the end of 1895 and, having an understanding with the local
chief constable, drove it quite often near his home. One day, however,
he unwisely ventured 3 miles over the Scottish border into Berwick-on-
Tweed, which resulted in a fine of sixpence with 19s 6d costs.

Such was the ludicrous attitude of English officialdom: strict enforce-
ment of the 4 mph speed limit, usually accompanied by the demand that
cars should be preceded by a man with a red flag, despite the fact that
this requirement had actually been dropped in 1878. This attitude
persisted for more than 10 years after Benz and Daimler had built their
first petrol-engined vehicles, and British motorists were still restricted
to a walking pace when the fastest French machines were averaging
anything up to 20 mph over some sections of their long-distance races.
Small wonder, then, that all the more significant advances in car design
emanated from France, and French words—chassis, chauffeur, garage,

*As a piece of automobile engineering
the contemporary Peugeot lagged
behind the Panhard, but in charm
and elegance it was unrivalled.*

accumulator, carburettor—studded the new motoring vocabulary.

The big French race of 1896 was even longer, a total of 1062·5 miles from Paris to Marseilles and back, but it was split into ten separate stages, Emile Levassor having declared that it was too dangerous to race after dark. For Levassor the race was in one sense a triumph, as the four-cylinder Panhard which he had designed won the event in the hands of Mayade. But Levassor himself overturned his own car near Orange and suffered internal injuries which eventually led to his death the following year at the age of 54. Despite the length of the course and appalling weather conditions, 15 of the 32 starters reached Marseilles and 14 completed the distance. This time only two steamers were entered and neither reached the finish; although steam cars were to prove extremely fast over shorter distances and remained popular with some users for years to come, they showed up poorly in town-to-town races until the pneumatic tyre was sufficiently improved to give these heavier vehicles a smoother ride, and by that time the petrol car was in an unassailable position.

Two more Panhards came second and fourth, but two of the little de Dion tricycles—generally regarded as mere playthings and entered only at the last minute—surprisingly finished third and fifth. Peugeot, now using an engine of their own manufacture, could manage no better than sixth place.

Racing and 'production' cars being virtually the same in those days, a closer look at the competing vehicles tells us what progress had been made in the first decade of motoring history. The winning four-cylinder Panhard had a wheelbase of only 5 feet 6 inches (the two-cylinder models were even shorter), the driver's seat was nearly 4 feet off the ground, and most of the weight was well above ground level, too. The wooden-spoked wheels (much larger at the back than in front) were shod with solid rubber tyres, there were no shock-absorbers, no self-centring or castor action was provided, and the steering was both direct and reversible. Combine these features with tiller control (still used then on most cars, although Panhard had experimented with wheel steering the previous year) and brakes that were quite hopelessly inefficient, and you have a device that will run away with you and overturn at the drop of a hat. Which, in fact, is exactly what many of them did, and the racing achievements of the period reflect far more credit on the drivers than on the vehicles they used.

Although the advantages of pneumatic tyres were beginning to be recognised, few racing drivers could accept the awful handicap of having

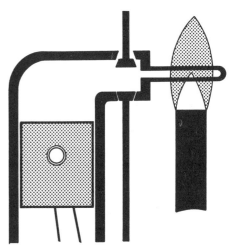

Daimler followed Levassor's lead by producing a four-cylinder engine in 1899. Instead of electric coil ignition (pioneered on the de Dion engine), the Daimler engine had tubes screwed into the cylinder-head and kept red-hot by burners placed outside in a separate metal box. When the piston rose, the gas was forced into contact with the hot tube and thus ignited.

The de Dion motor tricycle of the 1890s revealed a different approach. It offered neither elegance nor weather protection, but light weight and simplicity ensured a brisk and usually trouble-free performance.

Société Anonyme des VOITURETTES AUTOMOBILES LÉON BOLLÉE

163, Avenue Victor-Hugo.

PARIS

CONSTRUCTEUR-MÉCANICIEN

MOTEUR À PÉTROLE GAZ

FIXE

Mécanique de Précision

Fastest thing on wheels in the middle 1890s was the Léon-Bollée tri-car, capable of almost 30 mph. But the brakes and steering were something less than perfect, and the unfortunate passenger had a first-class view of the approaching accident.

to stop every few miles to repair punctures or replace burst tyres; even the solid rubber tyres had to be wired to the rim, and some still put their faith in iron-shod wheels despite the frightful pounding that resulted. Frequent halts were made to top up with cooling water, which simply boiled away because most cars had no radiators, or to lubricate the engine and transmission. Panhard had now started to enclose their drive gears, but many designers left the transmission—even the crank-shafts and big-end bearings—totally exposed, and therefore ball bearings were scarcely used at all. All the engines, single, twin or four-cylinder, ran so roughly that the whole car shook on its springs like a jelly.

They were almost completely inflexible, and governed to run at one particular speed. The inlet valves were 'atmospheric': that is, merely sucked open on the inlet stroke and closed again, more or less, by a light spring. Some had simple (and highly inefficient) carburetters, some were merely fed with petrol vapour from the top of the tank, and the idea of controlling engine speed by means of a throttle was thought quite wrong. Nor could the ignition timing be varied when the mixture was usually ignited by platinum tubes, kept permanently red hot by means of blowlamp-like burners outside the engine. In windy weather the burners frequently blew out. If the car overturned the burners would probably set light to the petrol and the whole thing would go up in flames. To many a sorely-tried driver, such an occurrence must have seemed a blessing in disguise.

In short, by the standards of today—indeed, by the standards of only 10 or 15 years later—early cars were mechanical abominations, uncomfortable, unreliable, and well-nigh uncontrollable. To leave it at that, however, is to make a false judgment by the standards of another time. It was quite different in the days when Queen Victoria had yet to celebrate her diamond jubilee, Oscar Wilde still languished in Reading Gaol, Marconi was still having an uphill struggle with his new wireless telegraphy, and music lovers were acclaiming the latest efforts of the Strauss family. Then, the criterion of cross-country personal transport (as distinct from transport *en masse* by railway train from one fixed point to another) remained the horse-drawn vehicle, which had colossal shortcomings completely unknown to most of us today. Compared with that, the motor-car had already revealed itself as a marvellous machine, docile, easily handled, comfortable, and capable of covering enormous distances at speeds which no horse-drawn device could possible equal.

Early Fiat advertisements suggested that in their cars the lady passenger could remain fashionably unruffled at all times. Even without a windscreen?

MAKING IT GO PROPERLY

There's nothing in the world to equal travelling in a motor-car. You can go fast or slow; you can stop where you like and as long as you like; with a little luggage on your car you're as independent as a bird; and like a bird you float through the air, with no thought for timetables.
C and A Williamson, *The Lightning Conductor*, 1902.
One hunts in cold, damp weather, and when it is dry and hot one motors. To each its appropriate time.
Mrs Edward Kennard, *The Lady's Pictorial*, 1905.

In the 30 years of greatest progress in motor-car design, no period is more significant than the middle decade. To apply just one very elementary rule of thumb: in 1896, about the fastest thing on wheels was the Léon-Bollée tricar, capable of something less than 30 mph; by the early part of 1906, an American steam car had added *almost one hundred miles an hour* to that figure. And if the Stanley Rocket was very much a 'special', all the best racing cars could easily (comfortably is definitely not the word) exceed 90 mph by that time.

The touring car, too, had changed considerably. In 1896, J.H. Knight had good reason to write: 'The present machines . . . are far from perfect, but they can undoubtedly be used by men who have a fair knowledge of mechanics.' Charles Jarrott put it more succinctly: 'It was impossible to know, when starting out on a journey, when or whether one would return.' Ten years later, long-distance touring by motor-car was a fashionable pursuit for the well-to-do, and many a stately horseless carriage was to be seen in the more expensive watering places of the Côte d'Azur.

The early development of the motor-car was accelerated and strongly influenced by the fact that a handful of manufacturers had thrown themselves wholeheartedly into the racing game, and at first no sharp distinction could be drawn between racing car and touring car: the three leading Panhards of the 1896 Marseilles race were bought by Charles

England's first motor show was staged in 1895 by Sir David Salomons, in the grounds of his Tunbridge Wells home. He is seen (left, in black homburg) demonstrating his Peugeot, one of the first cars to be seen in this country.

The first Wolseley, which appeared in 1896, was a tri-car rather like the Léon-Bollée, but it had a twin-cylinder engine and the driver (in this case the designer, Herbert Austin) sat at the front. The Chaplinesque figure is the passenger, who could see where he had been but not where he was going.

The ponderous Saurer, a little-known Swiss car of 1898, had a single-cylinder engine of more than 3 litres but could only manage about 12 mph flat out.

The 20 hp Rolls-Royce of 1905/6 was a very different proposition, and when the Hon. Charles Rolls broke the non-stop Monte Carlo to London 'record' with one of them, he averaged 27·3 mph for the first 771 miles to Boulogne. By then, cars were no longer mere horseless carriages.

Left: *the handsome 24 hp de Dietrich of 1902/3 was really a French Turcat-Méry built under licence in Alsace. This example, owned by an English gold-mining* pioneer, *was stored in London and forgotten for 46 years before being rescued by its owner's grandson.* Above: *while the de Dietrich was one of the costliest cars of its day, the* Darracq *was an inexpensive little machine, among the first to be built in large quantities. It had only a single-cylinder engine, but final drive by shaft instead of chain.*

Rolls, S.F. Edge and Charles Jarrott, who drove them regularly on the roads of England. In the first years of the new century it was racing that brought the Mercédès into existence, and its racing successes that made it a name to conjure with. Then, for a time, the situation changed because racing designers continually sought greater speed by making their engines bigger every year, instead of more efficient, so that the top cars no longer bore any resemblance to anything the ordinary man would have wanted to drive—or, indeed, could have driven. The Panhard that brought Emile Levassor home first in the 1895 Bordeaux race had a two-cyclinder engine of 1 206 cc, just about the capacity of a small popular car of today. The Grand Prix Panhard of 1906 was a night-marish monster of 18 279 cc—in other words, *each* of its four mammoth cylinders was bigger than most European car engines in general use nowadays. By then, even the French had begun to tire of motor racing in the grand manner. Other types of competition, and races for other types of car, were helping to develop qualities of more importance to the ordinary motorist. And gradually even Grand Prix racing changed, too, so that once again the competing cars represented the ultimate in motoring design.

In England, back in 1895 when a self-satisfied Establishment still placed every possible obstacle in the path of the would-be motoring enthusiast, there were just a few men perceptive enough to realise that the leading Continental car builders were developing a substantial export business and leaving British engineers out in the cold. Finding this state of affairs intolerable, they set about changing it.

The leading spirit was Sir David Salomons. In October 1895 he held an exhibition and demonstration of horseless carriages in the grounds of his home at Tunbridge Wells, and if the vehicles present could be counted on the fingers of one hand, they aroused much interest and were duly described in the first issue of *The Autocar*, which appeared on November 2. On December 10, Salomons formed the Self Propelled Traffic Association to campaign for more reasonable legislation. He had already succeeded in arousing some support in Parliament, but a change of government caused the project to be shelved for several months.

There were others who began to show a less altruistic interest, notably H.J. Lawson of safety bicycle fame, who saw in the new invention a chance to make a great deal of money for himself. To this end he formed the British Motor Syndicate to buy up the English rights

Scottish-born Alexander Winton was one of the first American car builders and designed some unusual racing cars, but his production models, like most American cars of the time, lagged behind European design. This 20 hp Winton of 1903 has a twin-cylinder engine mounted under the seats.

By contrast, the 18 hp Peugeot double phaeton of the same year (below) features a forward-mounted four-cylinder engine and fashionable honeycomb radiator, much more up-to-date than the Winton or the Delahaye of about the same period. Thirty years were to pass before the Delahaye became renowned as a fast and exciting car.

in the appropriate Continental patents, floated the (British) Daimler Motor Company, set up the Motor Car Club–an allegedly social organisation heavily subsidised by the Syndicate–and, in May 1896, organised a much grander exhibition than the humble Salomons affair. These moves, and many more, were all part of a plot to gain control of the infant British motor industry, and although Lawson's methods were as doubtful as his motives, he became a very big figure in the motoring world before eventually finding himself behind bars.

It is one of the mysteries of motoring history that the wily Lawson was himself taken in by an even smoother operator, an American named Pennington. This large and colourful character appeared in England with a sheaf of brochures describing a wide array of vehicles powered by the patent Pennington engine, whose peculiarities included a most eccentric ignition system and a complete absence of cooling system or carburetter. Some of these vehicles he undoubtedly built, and at least he was ahead of his time in fitting them with large-section pneumatic tyres that would scarcely have looked out of place on a modern car. But it was hard to swallow the assertion that his motor cycle had covered a mile in 58 seconds, or leapt 65 feet across a river. Yet Lawson paid him a cool £100 000 for his patent rights.

America also had her Lawson in the person of George B. Selden, who had gambled at exceedingly long odds by filing a vague patent application, relating to a motor carriage, as early as 1877. By various

One of the wilder claims of the remarkable Pennington : that one of his motorcycles had leapt 65 feet across a river !

No. 549,160.

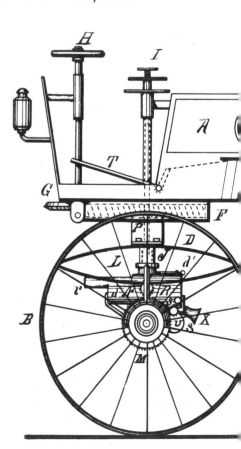

subterfuges he renewed his application at intervals until, on November 5 1895, he secured US Patent No. 549160. A few years later, when everyone realised that the horseless carriage definitely had a future, he was able to sell out to the American Association of Licensed Automobile Manufacturers. This body claimed that it was protecting the American car industry by restricting manufacture to those who were 'good and reliable', but its main activity was to demand a 1½ per cent royalty on gross sales from each new car builder. The Association successfully sued some manufacturers and gave sleepless nights to many others, but eventually it was beaten, primarily by the stubbornness of Henry Ford, and the Selden patent was shown to be worthless.

In January 1896 *The Autocar* inaugurated a petition to Parliament to 'allow light locomotives to run on the roads of the United Kingdom'. In February the Self Propelled Traffic Association presented a deputation with the same aim, and in March a bill was put before the House of Lords. On November 14 1896 the Light (Road) Locomotives Act came into force, and at last it was possible to use a motor-car in Britain without walking attendants or a 4 mph speed limit. There was still a limit, however; originally 14 mph, it had been trimmed to 12 mph by the time negotiations ended.

To Lawson and his Motor Car Club, this was the signal for a grand Emancipation Run to Brighton on that day, to show the public that a new age had dawned in England. By all accounts (and no two agree in

Overleaf: the first production Ford was the cheeky little Model A of 1903, an ultra-simple runabout with two seats, two cylinders, and two forward speeds. Yet it was far from being the cheapest car on the American market. In those days, a a Ford cost $100 more than a Cadillac.

In 1903 the Selden patent case was causing considerable worry to American car makers. The ALAM issued stern warnings in the motoring press, countered by reassurances from a defiant Henry Ford. The drawing of Selden's 'road engine' show how worthless his patent really was.

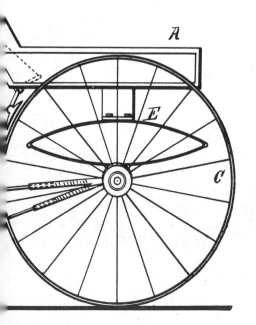

E.

Patented Nov. 5, 1895.

Fig. 1.

A

E

C

all respects) it was a chaotic performance. The pilot car was Levassor's 1895 Bordeaux-winning Panhard, 'Old Number 5', driven by Otto Meyer of the Daimler company and passengered by Lawson, whose garb (including the yachting cap favoured by Motor Car Club members) was such that he was likened to a Swiss admiral. Next came Gottlieb Daimler riding in a German Daimler driven by Van Toll, some French enthusiasts in the 1896 Marseilles-winning Panhard 'Number 6', driven by the winner of that race, Mayade, the the Hon. Evelyn Ellis' own Panhard, and Turrell, Lawson's secretary, in d'Hostingue's 1896 Marseilles Panhard. Nobody will ever know how many cars actually started and how many finished, but it seems clear that Lawson's Panhard had come to rest by Brixton Hill, whereupon the fierce little Léon-Bollée tricars proceeded to make a race of it.

Léon himself apparently reached Brighton first, averaging almost 15 mph for the 53 miles, but by 1905 an American writer was claiming that 'a yellow-wheeled Duryea car from a place well at the rear beat the French winners into Brighton by over an hour'. Yellow-wheeled or not, two of these American cars had indeed been sent over to take part in the event. Most reports say that one of them finished third, though there were doubts that it had gone all the way under its own power.

Some cars certainly did not. Almost 40 years later, at the official dinner following the annual Brighton Run of 1935, Walter Bersey disclosed that one of his electric broughams was put on a train at Redhill so that, carefully smeared with mud, it could make a triumphant appearance at the finish. At that same dinner the then Mayor of Brighton revealed that in 1896 he had been a newspaper reporter, and recalled that Lawson had issued a full report of the event (full of praise for the performance of his own car) on *November the thirteenth*.

The first Brighton Run, 1896. The two cars seen here at the London starting point are 'Old Number 5' and 'New Number 5', the racing Panhards driven by Levassor in the 1895 Paris-Bordeaux and 1896 Paris-Marseilles races. H.J. Lawson travelled in one and his secretary, McRobie Turrell, in the other.

Pennington got little further than Brixton before bursting one of his widely-advertised 'unpuncturable' tyres, and a Daimler delivery van, intended to serve as a breakdown tender, itself broke down so often that the unfortunate driver reached Brighton at three o'clock the following morning. It is doubtful if more than a third of the starters actually got there under their own steam, if at all.

So one can understand Jarrott's comment that 'after the procession to Brighton everybody, including even horse dealers and saddlers, relapsed into placid contentment, and felt secure that the good old-fashioned animal used by our forefathers was in no danger of being displaced.' Twelve months later, Lawson's South Sea Bubble was beginning to deflate, and his shareholders were very worried men. A disenchanted group of Motor Car Club members formed the Automobile Club of Great Britain and Ireland in December 1897, under the highly competent secretaryship of Claude Johnson. In 1898 the ACGBI (which in 1907 was to become the Royal Automobile Club) absorbed the Self Propelled Traffic Association, and thereafter concentrated on a series of tours and trials designed to reassure an understandably distrustful public.

In France, the Comte de Chasseloup-Laubat struck an unexpected blow for hot-water enthusiasts in January 1897 by winning the Marseilles-Nice race with his steam carriage. During this event, Fernand Charron, a newcomer to the Panhard team, turned a complete somersault and escaped serious injury by a miracle when he lost control of his car. On April 14 poor Levassor died from the results of his accident in the previous year's Marseilles race. Then, in a minor race at Périgeux in 1898, a driver and his mechanic were both killed. At last the car-builders realised something that should have been obvious long before, that reversible steering controlled by lever or tiller was much too dangerous now that speeds had risen. So almost everybody had steering wheels for the next big race. Panhard had now started using gilled-tube radiators as well, many of their components were made in aluminium, they had fitted pneumatic tyres, and generally improved the handling of their cars.

This new event was to be something special, a combined race and demonstration run from Paris to Amsterdam and back. It very nearly didn't happen, for at the last moment the Paris police chose to inspect all the competing cars for roadworthiness and refused to pass most of them. In the full-blooded Gallic row that followed, the police called out a company of infantry, half-a-squadron of the 23rd Hussars, and two field guns. The drivers promptly switched the starting point to Villiers, outside the jurisdiction of the Paris police, then realised that they had left their petrol supplies behind. However, Amédée Bollée made a daring raid on the enemy camp with a horse and cart, and all was well again. And Charron won the race for Panhard at 26·82 mph.

Among the cars that upset the Paris police engineer were some new boat-shaped models designed by Amédée Bollée Jr. Not long after this, his brother Léon designed a car for Darracq, and Décauville took a leaf from the Bollée book by building a car similar to Léon's famous tricar, but with two de Dion engines. Towards the end of 1898, Chasseloup-Laubat, switching from steam to electricity with a Jeantaud car, set up the first flying kilometre record—the first Land Speed Record, in fact—with an average of 39·3 mph. This led to a series of duels with Camille Jenatzy of Belgium,' who eventually built a new electric streamliner called the *Jamais Contente* and, on April 29 1899, achieved 65·75 mph. Nobody could fail to be impressed by this figure, which represented over 100 kph to the Continentals and more than a mile-a-minute to the English. Jenatzy, brave man that he was, controlled his lofty cigar-shaped projectile by means of a small tiller on the steering column.

New designs now began to appear in such profusion that we can mention only some of the more significant. A 21-year-old Louis Renault

'Do not take anything down unless you know what you are going to do with it when you have got it down.'

Comte de Dion's advice to a customer, 1899

Early perpendicular : Louis Renault, in 1899, was one of the first manufacturers to fit closed bodywork, but as his 2¼ hp chassis was rather short in the wheelbase, the result was distinctly peculiar.

SPYKER FWD, 1903

Some remarkably advanced cars were to be seen in the early years of the new century. Top: *the Dutch Spyker of 1903 was the first car in the world to have a six-cylinder engine, the first with four-wheel drive, and the first with braking to all four wheels.*
Above: *the 200 hp Darracq of 1905 had an ohv V-8 engine of no less than 22,518 cc, and set a new Land Speed Record of 109·65 mph.*

Above: *more than half a century before the Mini appeared, Walter Christie of New Jersey was building racing cars with transverse engines driving the front wheels, and he followed them in 1908 by this New York taxicab, which also had Lancia-style ifs before the Lancia did!*

Camille Jenatzy, later famous as a Mercédès team driver, sets out on the run to establish a new Land Speed Record of 65·75 mph with his electric streamliner on April 29 1899.

built himself a little tubular-chassis car with a secondhand ¾ hp de Dion tricycle engine at the front, a three-speed gearbox giving a direct-drive top and, for the first time, transmission through a universally-jointed propeller shaft to a sprung live axle. It was an immediate success, but nobody would have been more surprised than young Louis if told that he had just produced the transmission layout of the future. When de Dion himself announced his first four-wheeled petrol car a little later, he still had the engine at the rear, but there was an ingenious two-speed gearbox, with gears in constant mesh and engaged by expanding clutches which made the car easier to drive than most of its contemporaries. At first the rear end was unsprung, but de Dion soon reverted to an earlier layout by mounting the final drive on the chassis, with universally-jointed shafts to the wheels. This arrangement was much later to be adopted by the designers of some outstanding racing and sports cars. As for the de Dion Bouton car, it soon became a best seller, widely copied by other manufacturers.

Another advanced car was the Gobron-Brillié with its opposed-piston engine—that is, there were two pistons to each of its two cylinders. About the same time the first four-wheeled Wolseley appeared; hardly an advanced design this, with its horizontal single-cylinder engine, tiller steering and transmission by belt and chains. But it was built by a man named Herbert Austin, who had preceded it by two three-wheelers, the first obviously modelled on the Léon-Bollée.

The ancient Daimler wagonette was at last given Lankensperger steering and its engine moved to the front, Panhard style, while the Benz acquired a second cylinder. And Paul Daimler, son of Gottlieb, designed a 24 hp racing model for the Cannstatt organisation.

In America, Alexander Winton had sold one of his first cars to the Packard brothers, who used it as the starting point for a car built to their own design. Locomobile, who had bought the Stanley twins' rights to their steam car, started building in quantity and exported some of their steamers to England, where one of their customers was no less a personage than Rudyard Kipling. The Automobile Club of America was founded on June 7 1899 and held its first event in November; a 7-mile run, it was completed by fewer than a dozen of the 38 starters (it was said that at the time there were not more than 50 cars in the whole of the USA). Winton, with more patriotism than sense, issued a challenge to the great Fernand Charron, which led James Gordon Bennett of the *New York Herald* to offer a trophy for a series of international races.

During the very full season of French racing in 1899, it became obvious that Panhard no longer held undisputed sway. They now had larger engines, but so had Peugeot, while Mors, a newcomer two years before, had greatly improved their cars with the use of throttle valves and electric ignition. Peugeot won at Nice and Pau, Mors at St. Malo and Biarritz. In those days, cars were usually sent away from the line at intervals, but for the 200-mile Ostend race they all went off together, and this brought the first dead heat in motor racing when Girardot's Mors and Levegh's Panhard crossed the finishing line wheel-to-wheel. In the midst of this excitement hardly anyone noticed that a de Dion tricycle (which had been despatched *later*, with the other tricycles) had actually completed the distance in a shorter time. Two months earlier, when the Chevalier de Knyff won the mammoth 1350-mile Tour de France for Panhard at 30·2 mph, Teste's de Dion tricycle had come fourth at 26·5 mph. Racing cars were getting bigger, but perhaps there was something to be said for the light and simple vehicle.

The most amusing race of the year was a handicap event run between Paris and Trouville for walkers, horses, bicycles, motor tricycles and cars, which were allowed respectively 20, 14, 5, 3¼ and 3 hours to cover the 105-mile course. This handicapping brought a close finish in which the honours went to a nine-year-old mare followed by another horse, a de Dion tricycle, and a Mors.

By comparison with all this French activity the major British event of 1899, the ACGBI's first trials and motor show at Richmond Park, was small potatoes indeed, but one of the cars was of particular interest. Frederick Lanchester had built his first prototype in 1895, this one in 1897. A brilliant engineer, he had made a completely fresh approach in order to design a vehicle that would measure up to his own high standards, and it bristled with unusual features. Unable to accept the appalling vibration of most contemporary engines, Lanchester had built a twin-cylinder with two crankshafts which, geared together, turned in opposite directions to achieve unheard-of smoothness in running. There was a flywheel magneto, an epicyclic gearbox, and worm drive to the live rear axle. But if it had taken him four years and more to get this far, it took another four for his car—still further improved in detail—into production. Moreover, Lanchester stubbornly retained some features, like lever steering and a horizontal engine, that were considered very old fashioned by 1901. Above all, his cars *looked* peculiar, so they never found great favour with the public, although many of his ideas were later adopted by other designers.

In March 1900, shortly after the death of Gottlieb Daimler, several

Frederick Lanchester and his younger brother, George, in his second car, built in 1897. It won a gold medal at the ACGBI Richmond Park trials two years later, but production versions did not appear until 1901.

examples of his son's new racing model took part in the Nice–Marseilles event. They were certainly fast, with their 5-litre engine, and the new 'honeycomb' radiator attracted much attention, but they also gained a reputation for being distinctly dangerous, their bad handling qualities emphasising the Cannstatt firm's lack of racing experience. Several capable drivers got into trouble with them during the race, and Wilhelm Bauer crashed fatally at La Turbie. One driver was Emil Jellinek, an Austro-Hungarian diplomat with the odd but profitable sideline of selling expensive cars to expensive people in and around Nice, where he lived. He publicised this activity by calling his car a 'Mercédès' (actually the name of one of his daughters) instead of a Daimler, and even used the same pseudonym himself when racing; indeed, he had hopes of establishing a new company to market cars designed by Gottlieb Daimler's old partner, Wilhelm Maybach. This plan came to nothing, but he managed to arrange for Maybach to design and Cannstatt to build a completely new and even more powerful car in which he, Jellinek, would enjoy the sole selling rights.

Trouble blew up when the time came to pick the three French representatives for the new Gordon Bennett race, the rules stipulating that this was to be contested between teams of three drivers, each representing one country. Chosen by ballot, the three Frenchmen all turned out to be Panhard drivers, which left Peugeot and Mors out in the cold. However, there were only five starters for the race and Charron's Panhard easily won the Trophy for France, despite a tremendous crash when he hit a dog shortly before the finish. As for Alexander Winton, whose challenge to Charron had started the whole thing, his single-cylinder, tiller-steered car looked so ridiculous beside the European contenders that Charron said, 'It takes some cheek to come and race against us with a thing like that!'

The following month, more fuel was added to the row over selection when Levegh's Mors won the Paris–Toulouse–Paris race, at an average speed of 40·2 mph over 837 miles, compared with Charron's 38·6 mph for the mere 354 miles of the Gordon Bennett. The controversy on this topic was by no means over.

In 1900 Britain at last had her first long-distance motoring event. The British motor industry was still almost non-existent, and Claude Johnson conceived the idea of a 1000-Mile Trial which was 'organised with the object of advancing the automobile movement in the United Kingdom. This important branch of the engineering industry has already attained very considerable proportions on the Continent, where many thousands of men are engaged at high wages in the manufacture

There were few genuine British cars in Britain's first long-distance event, the 1000-Mile Trial of 1900. The leading car in this group of finishers is a Marshall dog-cart, an English copy of the Hurtu, which was a French copy of the Benz.

By 1901 the typical racing car had reached such proportions that Girardot's 40 hp Panhard was one of the smaller cars in the Paris-Bordeaux event. He finished tenth, but won the Gordon Bennett Trophy as the only survivor in that category.

The ladies soon began to take an active interest in motor sport, and some events were actually organised especially for them. Here the Duchess of Sutherland, in ultra-fashionable Mercédès, relegates her bowler-hatted companion to the passenger's seat and her chauffeur to the tonneau behind.

Car versus train: the Michelin tyre company celebrates Panhard's 'race' with the Paris-Calais express The driver was George Heath, an expatriate American who raced Panhards from 1898 to 1908.

of motor vehicles, the demand for which is far greater than the supply . . . The Committee of the Club are of the opinion that this kingdom should not remain, as it does at present, in the rear of the foreign countries as regards the new industry.' So an impressive route was planned with exhibitions staged at Bristol, Birmingham, Manchester, Edinburgh, Newcastle, Leeds and Sheffield, to give the great British public a chance to see what a harmless but useful animal the motor-car was.

Most of the cars they saw were necessarily foreign, however disguised by English name plates; they were English-assembled, or simply imported as complete vehicles. Sixty-five started, 17 retired, and 12 'maintained a speed throughout of not less than the legal limit', as the ACGBI coyly expressed it. The only genuine British makes among the finishers were Wolseley, Lanchester and Napier—and the latter owed its inspiration to Panhard. During S.F. Edge's ownership of his 1896 Paris-Marseilles car he had a new body fitted, pneumatic tyres, wheel steering, and eventually a new engine made for him by Montague Napier of Lambeth. A few months before the 1000-Mile Trial it had been agreed that Napier would build complete cars, Edge would sell them, and the financial backing would come from the Du Cros family (owners of Dunlop, the company that employed Edge). The first Napier, built for Edward Kennard, was hurriedly completed in time for the event and driven by Edge, who won the silver-gilt medal. Charles Rolls won the gold medal with his 12 hp Panhard, the little belt-driven Wolseley took the silver, and the ACF bronze medal went to the New Orleans, which, despite its American name, was a Twickenham-built version of the Belgian Vivinus (also known as a Georges Richard in France, a de Dietrich in Germany; there is nothing very new about the game of 'badge engineering').

In the autumn of 1900 the first American motor show was held at Madison Square Garden, and the White steam car went into production at Cleveland, Ohio; one of the most popular of all steam cars, it met with the approval of Theodore Roosevelt during his presidency. R.E. Olds started series production of his Oldsmobile, using engines made for him by Henry Leland, but refused an improved engine offered by the same designer. However, the Detroit Automobile Company liked it enough to join forces with Leland and produce a new car known as the Cadillac.

The new 35 hp Mercédès appeared early in 1901 but scored only one racing victory, the two most important races of the year going to Fournier's Mors. In 1900 the 5·9-litre Mercédès would have seemed a big car; in 1901 it was dwarfed by the 7·4 litres of the 40 hp Panhard, more than 10 litres of the 60 hp Mors, and no less than 17 157 cc in the case of Edge's huge racing Napier. No wonder *La France Automobile* referred to them scornfully as 'sortes de locomotives'. They were immensely heavy, and all the drivers had to stop frequently to change tyres—which makes their 50 mph-plus race averages even more impressive. But the Gordon Bennett race, held in conjunction with the Paris-Bordeaux event, was a failure. The only car to challenge the French, Edge's Napier, was so heavy that he had to change his Dunlop tyres for a French make; this was not only highly embarrassing for a Dunlop employee, but also disqualified him from competing for the Trophy. So the French had a walkover and the Gordon Bennett was won by Girardot's Panhard, only survivor of their Trophy team. Soon after this, the AC de France announced that a weight limit of 1 000 kg would be imposed for the 1902 season.

However, there was already some dissatisfaction with the way the sport was developing, and when a small boy was killed during the Paris-Berlin event the French government announced a complete ban on road racing. It is a little difficult to believe that the very next race to be held, less than 11 months later, was organised *by the French government*. But it was. The Ministry of Agriculture wanted to find new markets for French alcohol, and decided to emphasise its superiority over petrol by holding a race in which all the cars would run on this fuel. In this respect the 1902 Circuit du Nord was a flop, for it was found that they ran very badly on alcohol. To turn an ironic situation into pure comic opera, the second man home collided with the Commissaire of Police as he crossed the finishing line. It was certainly a day for red faces in official circles.

The weight limit also failed to achieve its object in one respect, for some of the new season's cars had even bigger engines than before. But at least designers were forced to give more thought to efficiency. Mors adopted a direct-drive top gear, like Renault, and for the first time fitted shock absorbers. Several followed the Mercédès in having their inlet valves mechanically-operated instead of atmospheric, for the German car had shown how smooth, quiet and flexible this made the engine when combined with electric ignition and throttle-valve control, and how much easier it was to change gear quickly with a 'gate' change and an engine that responded immediately to the throttle.

The new cars came out in force for the big race of 1902, over 615 miles from Paris to Vienna. Over the snow-covered Arlberg Pass, and

'When the car begins to slip backward on a steep grade, and you find you cannot control it, you had best jump out promptly and block the wheels with the biggest thing you can pick up quickly. If you prefer sticking to the tiller, steer the car as coolly as you can into some roadside obstacle.'

R.T. Sloss, *The Book of the Motor Car,* **1905**

The race that ended town-to-town racing was the 1903 Paris-Madrid, stopped at Bordeaux because so many were killed or injured. At that point Louis Renault (above, before the start) was lying second overall and leading his class when he learned that his brother, Marcel (left), had been fatally injured on the way. Fernand Gabriel (right) started late and passed 79 other competitors with his 70 hp Mors, to take 15 minutes off Louis' time in the 30 hp Renault, being thus declared the winner at Bordeaux.

on the rough roads of Austria, some of the smaller ones proved faster than the monsters, so that Marcel Renault's 3758 cc car and Count Zborowski's 6785 cc Mercédès both finished ahead of Farman's 13672 cc Panhard. A further surprise came in the Gordon Bennett contest, run concurrently with the big race, for the only survivor was Edge's 6·5-litre Napier, a real lightweight compared with his elephantine car of the previous year.

Six months later Count Zborowski was dead, killed on the La Turbie hill at the very point where Bauer had died when driving the 24 hp Daimler, predecessor of the Mercédès. But there was worse to come. The 1903 racing Panhards still had engines of more than 13½ litres capacity, Mors and de Dietrich both had about 11½ litres, and the new 90 hp Mercédès was fitted with a 12711 cc engine. The fastest cars were capable of almost 90 mph, but frames, springs, wheels and other components were all whittled to the minimum to meet the 1000 kg weight limit; they were little more than huge engines in stripped chassis fitted with bare seats. On such contraptions the competitors were expected to drive from Paris to Madrid for the main race of 1903, down the tree-lined roads of France and right through northern Spain. Each car travelled in a thick cloud of dust; to overtake, between the trees, was to play a grim game of Russian roulette.

And an estimated three million spectators flocked to watch the first day's racing, to line the roads and make them even narrower. Most of them had not the slightest notion of the danger involved; a speed of 80 mph was as far beyond their comprehension as the speed of a spaceship is to us today. 'I tried slowing down,' wrote Charles Jarrott, the first

'Red Devil' Jenatzy is congratulated on winning the 1903 Gordon Bennett in Ireland. His Mercédès is a stripped 60 hp touring model, the 90 hp racing cars having been destroyed in a factory fire.

man to leave the start, 'but quickly realised that the danger was as great at 40 mph as at 80. It merely meant that the crowd waited a longer time on the road.'

So there were many terrible accidents, some fatal, involving drivers (Marcel Renault was among those who died), mechanics, officials and spectators. The race was stopped at Bordeaux, where the surviving cars were towed away by horses. Fastest man over that first section of 342 miles was Fernand Gabriel with his Mors at 65·3 mph, and it is recorded that he overtook 79 other cars on the way.

Under the Gordon Bennett rules, each race had to be organised by

The 1903 Mercédès victory meant that the 1904 Gordon Bennett race was held in Germany, and the 75 hp Fiats which represented Italy closely resembled the successful German car. Race day was declared a public holiday, and the local populace took a lively interest in everything.

the national club of the previous winner. After Edge's 1902 victory the next race in the series should have been held in England, which was obviously impossible with a 12 mph speed limit still in force. Instead, a suitable course had been found in Ireland, and all the preliminary arrangements (including a special Act of Parliament) had fortunately been completed before the disastrous Paris-Madrid race was run. France was represented by two 80 hp Panhards and a 70 hp Mors, America by two Wintons (one of 40 hp rating, one of 80 hp) and an 80 hp Peerless, Britain by three Napiers, an 80 hp and two 45 hp.

Germany had intended to send three of her 90 hp Mercédès, but had to substitute three stripped 60 hp touring cars when the bigger cars were destroyed by a factory fire. This calamity was a blessing in disguise for Cannstatt. Jenatzy's car won the Trophy, and all the world took note of the way this splendidly-built touring car had beaten the specialised racing machines. Among those who had no need to count their pennies, a Mercédès 60 became *the* car to drive.

Although many smaller cars still had single-cylinder engines–notably the de Dion Bouton, now with its engine at the front and, on the larger 8 hp model, a three-speed gearbox–there was a growing demand for smoothness, and some designers had even produced eight-cylinder engines; one of the Wintons in the 1903 Gordon Bennett race had such a power unit. At the 1903 Paris Motor Show the Dutch Spyker appeared with a six-cylinder engine, four-wheel drive and front brakes on the drive shaft. Napier, too, started work on a six-cylinder 30 hp model that year, while a very skilled electrical engineer named Frederick Royce was amusing himself in Manchester by thinking out improvements to a 10 hp Décauville. Charles Rolls had just gone into business (later joined by Claude Johnson) to sell foreign cars in London, and in 1904 he was persuaded to go and meet Royce, who by this time had produced a little car to his own design. It was a perfectly conventional car, but it was also perfectly made. H. Massac Buist, who rode in it about the same time, later wrote: 'Needs one had never realised were herein anticipated, and a new standard of performance set.' Rolls was no less impressed, and encouraged Royce to build a range of other models as well, one of them a 30 hp six-cylinder, in time for the next Paris Show. Royce agreed. He agreed, too, that all these cars should be sold by Rolls in London under the name of Rolls-Royce.

The year 1904 was a notable one in several other respects. On

Charles Rolls breaks out in a rash of alliteration in one of his advertisements about 1906. Engine flexibility was considered a great virtue in those days.

One of the three cars built by Frederick Royce before he met Charles Rolls. It was a simple little 10 hp two-cylinder machine, quite conventional but beautifully made.

January 1, under the terms of a new Motor Car Act, cars on British roads were required to carry registration numbers and their drivers to be licensed, but to sugar the pill somewhat, the speed limit was raised to 20 mph–at which figure it remained for no less than 26 years. Henry Ford, driving his 'Arrow' special on a frozen Michigan lake, was timed at 91·37 mph the same month. On July 17, Louis Rigolly became the first man to top the 'century' when his 15-litre Gobron-Brillié recorded 103·56 mph at Ostend.

New makes to appear during the year included Chadwick, Crossley, Delaunay-Belleville, Maxwell, Vauxhall and Wolseley-Siddeley. Although the disaster of Paris-Madrid had put an end to town-to-town racing, the Gordon Bennett event was still held, over four laps of a dust-proofed and well-guarded circuit in Germany. It attracted entries from Britain, France, Germany, Austria, Belgium, Italy and Switzerland (although the Swiss car, being over the weight limit, did not start). Despite all the efforts of 'Red Devil' Jenatzy with his 90 hp Mercédès, the Trophy was won by a comparatively small car, Théry's Richard-Brasier, representing France.

The famous Panhards were not even selected for the French team, trouble with a new vee-shaped radiator having put them out of the eliminating trials, which were held on a tarred road, lined with spectator barriers, in a remote part of the Ardennes. The ACGBI, casting around for somewhere to hold the English eliminating trials, made the interesting discovery that the Isle of Man authorities were not averse to motor racing. The Americans did not enter at all, for they had a new inter-

At the London Motor Show of 1905, Rolls did not put all his eggs in one basket. There was a Rolls-Royce on display, but a prominent position on his stand was occupied by the 15 hp Orleans, another make for which he had a selling agency.

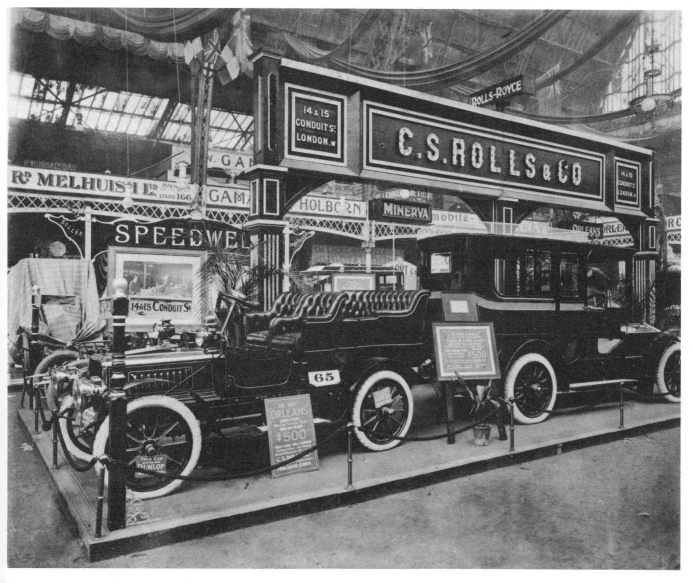

national race of their own that year, the Vanderbilt Cup event on Long Island, and Panhard had the consolation of winning this. A Pope-Toledo would have come third, but could not reach the finishing line because the crowds swarmed over the track, an occurrence that was to become something of a tradition in the Vanderbilt Cup series.

The 1904 Gordon Bennett having been the best so far, with 19 entries representing seven nations, it was unfortunate that the old trouble over French representation now blew up again. The French pointed out that they had had 29 entries for their eliminating trials, in 10 different makes

of French car, whereas other nations had difficulty in producing a three-car team at all. Therefore, they said, either they should be allowed a bigger team than the others, or the race should be run on an entirely different basis. Nobody else would accept this, so the French reluctantly went ahead with organising the 1905 race under the original rules. There were 18 entries, Belgium and Switzerland dropping out but America returning to the fray with two Pope-Toledos and a Locomobile (petrol, not steam). France was represented by two Brasiers and an enormous 17-litre de Dietrich rated at 130 hp (but even this would have been dwarfed by the 26 400 cc Dufaux of Switzerland, which did not materialise). Théry's Brasier won again for France, but two of the FIAT 110 hp models finished second and third, showing that while Italy had come late to motor racing, she was now a power to be reckoned with.

This was the last Gordon Bennett race, for it was obvious that the winning nation would not organise another. Like the French town-to-town races the 1900/1905 Gordon Bennett series had played an important part in the development of the motor-car, even if the giant racers were now heading in quite the wrong direction, and in particular provided an international yardstick against which the competing nations could measure the performance of their cars. National pride did the rest, forcing each country to improve its designs, and the American team cars of 1905 were a very different proposition from the old-fashioned Winton of 1900. Other races, too, encouraged designers to think up new ideas. Walter Christie's entry for the 1905 Vanderbilt Cup race had a transverse four-cyclinder engine driving the front wheels—more than half-a-century before the Issigonis Mini came out with this 'new' layout.

The ever-increasing reliability of the motor-car also encouraged long-distance touring by individuals or motor-club members, and pioneering cross-country journeys by the more adventurous. When Dr Nelson Jackson crossed the American continent in his Winton during the summer of 1903, 20 of his 65 days were devoted to repair work. A month later, Thomas Fetch and his Packard could only trim his time down to 61 days for the 4500 miles from San Francisco to New York, but in 1904, L.L. Whitman in a Franklin did it in 33 days. By then, C.J. Glidden was engaged in his round-the-world trip by car, and the trophy he presented to the American Automobile Association started the excellent Glidden Tours held annually until 1913.

When 75 cars started on a 500-mile run from New York to Boston and back in 1902, no less than 58 dropped out on the way; in the 1904 run from New York to St. Louis, more than three times the distance, a bare half-dozen of the 80 competitors had to retire. In 1905 an Indian motor club arranged a run from Delhi to Bombay, the Dunlop company organised one from Sydney to Melbourne, and Professor Herkomer offered a trophy (not to mention a portrait of the winner, painted by the professor himself) for a touring competition organised by the Bavarian Automobile Club.

These touring events also had their influence upon car design. So did another competition first held in 1905 which, although a motor race, was very different from the French interpretation of that word. The ACGBI called it the Tourist Trophy to emphasise that it was intended to develop touring cars, not mammoth racers. To make quite sure, they required all competing cars to carry full four-seater bodywork and allowed only a limited amount of fuel. The course they chose was in the Isle of Man, where the Club had enjoyed such a welcome for their Gordon Bennett eliminating trials in 1904. This time the reception was even more enthusiastic; finding that there were several level crossings included in the circuit, the Manx government obligingly stopped all train services on race day!

The fuel limitation effectively kept monster cars out of the TT and

Long-distance events were all the rage in America by 1905. Here, two curved-dash Oldsmobiles, the most popular car of their time in the USA, leave New York City to race 4000 miles to Portland, Oregon. The trip took 44 days.

the first race aroused little interest on the Continent, although several foreign cars were entered by their English concessionaires. The 42 starters also included Napier, Wolseley, Vauxhall, and two of the new Rolls-Royces, both rated at 20 hp although their engine capacities varied slightly (horsepower ratings were somewhat vague in those days); they also had four-speed gearboxes with a geared-up top. A rare example of pilot error by Charles Rolls put the bigger car out with a broken gearbox on the first lap, and the race was won by one of the highly unconventional opposed-piston Arrol-Johnstons from Scotland, with the remaining Rolls-Royce second and a Vinot et Déguingand third. The TT had certainly helped to bring some new names into the limelight, and when a Light Twenty Rolls-Royce finished well ahead of two French cars to win the 1906 race, its backers were able to float a public company and build a new factory at Derby.

In those days, of course, Rolls-Royce were some way from the top of the luxury car bracket. Even with the most expensive bodywork a 30 hp Rolls could be bought for about £1 000. The equivalent Napier, Panhard or de Dietrich cost over £1 300, their larger models very much more. A 60 hp Spyker cost £1 600, and a 60 hp Mercédès cost over £2 000 without any body at all.

The not-so-rich could putter about in any number of little cars costing £200 or less: a de Dion *Populaire,* Oldsmobile 7, Belsize Junior, Baby Peugeot or Rover 8. These could not cover enormous distances and they had to shed their passengers on almost every hill, but it must have been comforting for their owners to reflect that their purchase

In Edwardian times, motoring was a splendid pastime for those who could afford a high-quality car. They could thunder over the snow in a powerful open tourer, with costly furs to keep out the cold, or bowl along the boulevards in a stately landaulet with chauffeur and footman in attendance. Both of these cars are Fiats; they show how Ing. Enrico, the Fiat designer of that time, was greatly influenced by Mercédès practice.

price would not have kept the luxury carriages in tyres for six months.

When the first London Motor Show to be held at Olympia opened in 1905, there were 434 different types of car to choose from. In America alone there were 204 different models on the market, not counting foreign imports, at prices ranging from $375 for an Orient Buckboard to $6000 for a Peerless Model 12, Thomas Model 27, Locomobile Model H or Pope-Toledo Model 9.

The motor-car, then, however imperfect still, had undoubtedly taken its place in the social scene, and a contemporary writer was moved to poetic heights as he speculated upon its influence in 1905. 'The wand of its power,' wrote Filson Young, 'has touched the winds to a greater energy, so that the very air it consumes is crushed upon it with a prodigal bounty, sweetened with all the mingled perfumes of the fields and the seasons. It flattens out the world, enlarges the horizon, loosens a little the bonds of time, sets back a little the barriers of space. And man, who created and endowed it, who sits and rides upon it as upon a whirlwind, moving a lever here, turning a wheel there, receives in his person the revenues of the vast kingdom it has conquered. He lives more quickly for its vitality, drawing virtue and energy from its ardent heart . . .'

Mr Young, it is clear, never had the misfortune to swelter in a ten-mile traffic jam along the Brighton road on a hot Sunday in summer, the air about him filled with nothing sweeter than carbon monoxide. Such doubtful pleasures of motoring still lay in the remote future during the early years of the 20th century.

MAKING IT GO BEAUTIFULLY

Everyone in a certain position nowadays is expected to own a car, just as he is expected to live in a nicely furnished house, and it is important that his motor-car should be in keeping with the other possessions that from time to time he invites his friends to share . . . If one's only idea is to have a machine that will go along somehow, it is not likely that more money would willingly be spent for the refinement of smooth motion. It is rather like being satisfied, however, with any sort of piano that will make a noise.
A.E. Berriman, *Motoring*, 1914.

It is generally agreed that until about 1909, motoring remained primarily a pastime for the rich. True, many small and cheap cars were built in their thousands before this time, but they were not really practical vehicles in the sense that they would go anywhere and do anything. Writing of such models as the little de Dion Bouton and others in 1905, Filson Young said: 'It cannot be too clearly understood that the sport or hobby of driving these small machines is entirely distinct from that of motoring proper . . . In my opinion, the real use for these light cars, so far as distance is concerned, is much the same as that to which an expert and trained cyclist would put his bicycle . . .' The cars that 'went beautifully' before the First World War were bought by the gentry, not the Joneses. They were expensive touring models closely related, at first, to the successful racing cars that were built almost regardless of cost. Then, as Grand Prix racing went its own way, other influences affected the design of the best touring cars and refined them in a way that racing alone could never have done. Eventually John Citizen found some of the refinements on his own humble vehicle, but he had to wait a long time for them.

With so much difference between the two ends of the scale it is hard to decide what is truly representative of contemporary car design around 1906. We might say that the typical medium-powered car had a four-cylinder petrol engine in a pressed-steel chassis, with semi-elliptic leaf springs, no shock absorbers, and non-detachable wooden wheels fitted with beaded-edge pneumatic tyres. There was a foot brake working on the transmission and a hand brake working on the back wheels—not too effectively, so there was probably a 'sprag' to prevent the car running backwards downhill. The foot-operated clutch might be of cone or plate type. The separate three-speed gearbox had a right-hand lever working in a gate, and the final drive was probably by side chains. Though a fashionable honeycomb radiator might give a touch of Merc-like elegance, the inlet valves could be mechanically operated or merely atmospheric. The petrol tank, under the driver's seat, fed an updraught spray carburettor by gravity. On the low wooden dashboard was an oil tank, pressurised (by air pump or exhaust gas) so that the oil passed through a row of adjustable sight feed lubricators on the driver's side of the dash, and thence to the various points that needed it. For some extraordinary reason that elementary device, the dipstick, had not been thought of, and the oil level in the sump was anybody's guess.

Tube ignition had completely given way to electric, but many different systems were in use: low-tension magneto with mechanically-operated 'jump-spark' igniters in the cylinders; battery, sparking plugs and 'single-spark' coil with contact breaker, or trembler coils with

'By hook or by crook we must first ascertain how much oil there is in the crank chamber. Usually some form of inspection plate is fitted, and if this be in position on our car it must be removed, so that we can see whether the connecting rod ends are actually dipping into the oil at the lowest point of their movement. But supposing no inspection plate be fitted. We must in that case pour oil into the crank chamber by any available passage or opening, or even by setting the drips to run very freely, and continue to supply in this way until a suggestion of smoke is apparent from the exhaust when the engine is running freely at 500 r.p.m., we will say.'

The Autocar, **March 12, 1910**

Even in pre-war days, humour sometimes featured in motor advertising. Above: the French motoring artist, René Vincent, depicts a neat piece of one-upmanship by the ladies in their dashing Berliet roadster. Left: Gerald Smith even pokes fun at police speed traps in an advertisement for the Scottish-built Argyll car.

MY. WHAT A BEAUTY!
I BET THAT'S AN
ARGYLL.

The elegant and handsome bodies of the Argyll Cars are well in keeping with that perfection of mechanism which has made the reputation of

The FAMOUS ARGYLL.

Made only from the best selected materials, finished in the highest class style, and upholstered in leather and best quality horsehair, they present a perfect example of the coach-builder's craft.

Over a dozen types of bodies are made, amongst which the most fastidious will have no difficulty in making a satisfactory choice.

ARGYLL MOTORS, Ld., ALEXANDRIA, by GLASGOW.
London Agents: ARGYLLS, LONDON, LTD., 17, Newman Street, Oxford Street, W.

contact *maker* or 'wipe contact'; low-tension magneto replacing battery; high-tension magneto incorporating contact-breaker and distributor, feeding current direct to the sparking plugs. Jump-spark igniters, being inside the combustion chambers, needed frequent attention. Batteries had to be recharged daily, since there was no dynamo.

To start the engine you swung the starting handle. There was probably a centrifugal governor to hold the engine at its designed running speed, and a pedal to put the governor out of action; this was therefore called the accelerator, which is what we loosely (and incorrectly) call the throttle pedal today. At first it was considered bad driving to make constant use of the accelerator, which was reserved as a sort of awful threat to be employed on the steepest hills, and speed was largely controlled by hand-levers which advanced the ignition timing and opened a throttle valve. But one can hardly generalise: a contemporary driving manual lists *seven* different methods of controlling the speed.

Bodywork was minimal and offered scarcely any weather protection. Doors, windscreen, hood, lamps (acetylene or oil) and speedometer were all regarded as extras. Automatic wipers and rear-view mirrors did not exist at all.

On the unsealed road surfaces of the period, cars like these left a choking cloud of dust to mark their passage—far more than a few years earlier when speeds were lower, cars higher and tyres very much thinner. They took their toll of the cats, dogs, hens, cows and sometimes people that still wandered in leisurely fashion about the country lanes. The pioneer motorist had few friends, and in England the rural bobby gleefully set up speed traps to pull him in when he exceeded 12 mph–often, indeed, when he had not, for unjust prosecutions were commonplace. Yet the widespread resentment of the motor-car is easily understood. Many motorists *were* shamefully arrogant or inconsiderate in their behaviour, and it is noticeable that in the cars of that period the horn bulb is always in a much more accessible position than the brake lever.

The driver of such a car, capable of perhaps 35 mph flat out, must have been startled indeed in January 1906 to learn that Frank Marriott's streamlined Stanley steam car had recorded 127·66 mph on Daytona Beach. The first Targo Florio was run in Sicily, and the first French Grand Prix was held at Le Mans as a replacement for the discarded

When small cars began to feature in European racing, the most successful French make between 1906 and 1909 was the Sizaire-Naudin, an odd-looking machine with transverse-leaf ifs (right).

The six-cylinder Thomas Flyer (right, below) has long been considered one of the greatest American cars. It was a 72 hp model like this that Roberts and Schuster drove to victory in the 1908 race from New York to Paris, covering more than 12,000 miles (via Seattle, Japan and Siberia) in 170 days.

At the normal speed of an Edwardian barouche, you could tear each other's wheels off without much damage to the rest of the carriage. This brief encounter occurred in 1908.

Gordon Bennett series. This race showed what proportions the tyre problem was reaching; the Panhards and de Dietrichs had engines of more than 18-litre capacity, but first place went to a 12·9-litre Renault which had detachable rims to its wheels, so that tyre changes could be made more quickly (the bigger cars, perilously close to the 1 000 kg limit, could not afford the extra weight of the new rims they so sorely needed).

Another new French race, organised by the journal *l'Auto*, was for much smaller cars defined by engine bore, but not capacity, which was to give rise to some odd power units; it was won by an unusual vehicle with independent front suspension and a 1 357 cc engine, a Sizaire-Naudin, which was to win again in 1907 and 1908. The runner-up in the Vanderbilt Cup race, Fiat driver Vincenzo Lancia, decided to go into business as a car manufacturer himself. So did Herbert Austin, who left the Wolseley company and cycled around the outskirts of Birmingham until he found a factory site at a place called Longbridge. A 23-year-old Laurence Pomeroy joined Vauxhall Motors, whose products had so far attracted little attention, as assistant to the chief engineer.

Métallurgique of Belgium marketed a handsome 60/80 car which had a dynamo as a standard fitting. The Berliet, a French car in the Mercédès manner which ran second to the winning Rolls-Royce in the 1906 TT, was taken up by the American Locomotive Company and sold as the Alco. At the 1906 Olympia Motor Show, Rolls-Royce presented a new six-cylinder 40/50 car that was to win everlasting fame as the Silver Ghost. Its 7·4-litre engine was in effect two three-cylinder engines, a layout giving much smoother running than the three two-cylinder engines which made up Napier's six, and although the power output was

Hotchkiss of France were famous for their guns (like Maxim, FN and BSA) before turning to cars in 1903. They took an early interest in racing and successfully returned to motor sport in the 1930s with three Monte Carlo Rally victories.

Over the years, few cars have been more successful as a town carriage than the 20/30 hp Renault, with its distinctive radiator behind the bonnet. Many were used as taxis. In a vehicle that is 8 feet high you can really enjoy the view.

Interest in smaller cars was growing by about 1910, when Zuccarelli won the Coupe de l'Auto with a 2·6-litre Hispano-Suiza and finished third in the Catalan Cup Race (above) with a slightly smaller-engined model.

a mere 48 bhp (less than that of a modern Mini), Royce's painstaking attention to detail and superb standards of assembly made the Mercédès seem rough and clumsy by comparison. As Laurence Pomeroy Jr. has remarked, Frederick Lanchester designed the first scientific 20th-century car in the latter part of the 19th century; Frederick Royce produced the pinnacle of 19th-century mechanical design in the early part of the 20th century.

Napier hit the headlines when the new Brooklands circuit was opened the following June, S.F. Edge driving a 60 hp model single-handed for 24 hours at an average speed of 65·9 mph. He did it despite heavy rain and frequent tyre trouble, and caused so much damage to the 'green' concrete surface that cynics dubbed the new track the 'Edgewear Road'. Felice Nazzaro's Fiats dominated the major races of 1907, winning the Targa Florio in Sicily, Germany's one and only Kaiserpreis race, and—at 70·6 mph—the French GP, run under the fuel-consumption limit in an unsuccessful attempt to reduce engine sizes. The AC de France had made their fuel allowance too generous, unlike the TT organisers, who kept theirs so low that only two of the 22 starters finished the race at all. Still, the erstwhile ACGBI could bask in the glory of having become the Royal Automobile Club under the patronage of Edward VII. The monarch's enthusiasm for motoring might almost have made it seem respectable to the English, had not so many of his other activities been so obviously far from respectable.

Another monarch, Alfonso XIII of Spain, favoured the Hispano-Suiza although its designer, Marc Birkigt, was actually Swiss. Louis Coatalen, an expatriate Frenchman who had designed a 25 hp Hillman for the 1907 TT (and, incidentally, married Miss Hillman) decided to join Sunbeam. Lorraine-Dietrich of France partly took over Isotta-Fraschini of Italy, whose very advanced cars (their valves operated by overhead camshafts) attracted much attention; some said they were designed by an Italian-born engineer, Ettore Bugatti, who had worked for de Dietrich, Hermès and Deutz.

An extraordinary race was staged between Peking and Paris, attracting five starters of which the winner, Prince Scipione Borghese, covered 10 000 miles in 44 days with his Itala. There was even a race between St Petersburg and Moscow in 1907 and 1908, and a highly unsuccessful race from New York to Paris in 1908.

France having switched from Gordon Bennett races to Grands Prix to demonstrate her superiority in racing, it had been somewhat galling that an Italian car had won the 1907 Grand Prix. It was worse still when German cars, a Mercédès and two Benzes, took the first three

'No longer do we say with awe that So-and-so has a motor; on the contrary, we murmur sympathy, with a sad shaking of the head, when we are pointed out a person who still persists in keeping horses.'

Owen John, *The Autocar*, **March 13, 1912**

places in the 1908 event. It was particularly exasperating for the French because a French car, the ohc Clément-Bayard, was almost certainly the fastest in the race, timed at 104·8 mph—but it stopped 19 times for tyre changes, the Mercédès only nine times. And all the cars in the race could have had the new detachable wheels which had recently become available, but the AC de France had refused to allow competitors to use them.

Like the French GP, the 1908 TT was run under a restriction on bore diameter. It was won by Watson's Hutton (actually a Napier; the voluble Edge had so extolled his six-cylinder engine that he had to market his four-cylinder models under a different name). The RAC also ran a 2000-Mile Trial won by a Vauxhall 20, designed by Pomeroy while their chief engineer was on a trip abroad. Rolls-Royce won the Scottish Trial, and in the Bombay-Kholapur Trial one of their cars covered 620 miles with a locked bonnet, carrying neither tools nor spares. The Herkomer Trials were succeeded by a new competition, under the patronage of Prince Henry of Prussia, intended to improve

The great Ettore Bugatti brought out the Type 13 (above), *his first production model, with an ohc engine of 1·3-litre capacity.*
Bugatti also designed the delightful 'Bébé' (below) *which Peugeot brought out in 1912/13. It weighed less than 8 cwt, was less than 9 feet long, and its four-cylinder engine was of only 856 cc capacity.*

Ultimate automobiles. Left: *Rolls-Royce Silver Ghost, with under-bonnet view of a later type below.* Above: *one of the Mercédès team cars that ran in the 1908 French Grand Prix.*

the design of touring cars. The world's first supercharged car, a six-cylinder Chadwick, was seen in the new American Grand Prize race at Savannah; the winner was Wagner's Fiat, but the Chadwick won the Giant's Despair hill climb, and America enjoyed her first international race victory when Robertson's Locomobile won the Vanderbilt Cup.

America was now very prominent in the motoring world, her car production having exceeded that of France in 1906. Then, in October 1908, Henry Ford produced his amazing Model T, the ultra-simple and almost totally indestructible vehicle which eventually brought reliable motoring within nearly everybody's reach. Early in 1909 Ford dropped all his other models, and built 10 000 of the Model T in one year. More than that, he increased production every subsequent year and repeatedly reduced the price. In 1909–10 he sold 18 664 cars at $950; in 1916–17, 785 432 at a mere $360 apiece. When the Model T was eventually dropped in 1927, more than 15 million had been made.

American influence was also to be found in the English Daimler of 1909, for its double sleeve valve engine had been designed by Charles Yale Knight, who had previously tried unsuccessfully to interest his fellow countrymen in this mechanism. Another American enthusiast, Carl Fisher, managed to attract enough backing to build a circuit at Indianapolis. At the first meeting the track began to disintegrate, so before the end of the year it was resurfaced with bricks.

In Europe, however, there was something of a trade recession. Possibly for this reason, possibly because of the recent eclipse of French cars in racing, most manufacturers agreed not to race and so few entries were received for the French Grand Prix that it had to be cancelled, and it was not run again until 1912. The TT was also dropped, until 1914. But the Coupe de *l'Auto* series was now firmly established, and although it had developed some freak long-stroke designs at first, new regulations encouraged the entry of some really excellent small-capacity cars. One such was Zuccarelli's Hispano-Suiza which won the 1910 event at 55·6 mph with a side valve engine of only 2 646 cc–very different from the giant racers of the Grands Prix a couple of years before. There was, indeed, a growing interest in smaller cars, and Bugatti started his own company to market an ohc four-cylinder of 1 327 cc. For Peugeot he designed the minute Bébé, smaller again with an engine of only 856 cc.

After Ransom E. Olds left Oldsmobile in 1904 (giving his name, or rather his initials, to another American car, the Reo) the company built much larger cars than their famous little runabout. This handsome touring model was in production when General Motors took over in 1909.

In England, a tax on horsepower was introduced, and the first cyclecars began to appear, following the example set by the French Bédélia. But de Dion Bouton, famous for their small cars, announced a big luxury car with a vee-eight engine, later copied by Cadillac.

BSA bought the English Daimler company, Maybach left the Cannstatt Daimler firm to build cars under his own name, and the Austrian Daimler company entered a team of splendid 5·7-litre ohc cars in the Prince Henry Trial of 1910. Designed by Dr Porsche (later responsible for the sports Mercédès, the racing Auto Union, the Volkswagen and other famous cars), the Austro-Daimlers were capable of 88 mph at an engine speed of 2300 rpm and finished 1–2–3, the winning car driven by Porsche himself. In the same event, Vauxhall entered a team of 3-litre cars developed from a 1908 model. They were notable for their sleek and handsome bodywork, and their side valve engines made for a surprising turn of speed. Shortly after the 1910 Prince Henry Trial the first Austrian Alpine Trial was held, and this event also exercised a strong influence on the design of high-performance touring cars.

With a mammoth 21½-litre Blitzen Benz, the cigar-chewing Barney Oldfield topped 130 mph at Daytona. Harry Grant's Alco won the Vanderbilt Cup for the second successive year, but this event was over-shadowed by the American Grand Prize. For this, in 1910, a new course had been laid out, and a special enclosure was set aside for the convict labourers who had worked on it so that they could watch the fun. The winning Benz was driven by a remarkable youngster, the 20-year-old David Bruce-Brown, who won again the following year with a Fiat, but was tragically killed during practice for the 1912 event.

In July 1910 a 65 hp Napier was driven from London to Edinburgh and back in top gear, averaging 19·35 mpg, and then recorded 76·42 mph at Brooklands. Charles Rolls, who had for some time been more interested in aviation, was killed in a flying accident that same month. But the company he had founded felt compelled to hit back at their

In 1909 the English Daimler company adopted an American invention, the sleeve-valve engine, and used it until the early 1930s in a wide variety of cars which changed but little over the years. They built their own coachwork, such as this Edwardian landaulet, and found great favour with the Royal Family.

Cars for the not-so-rich. Left: a restored 1910 example of Henry Ford's famous Model T, of which more than 15 million were built between 1908 and 1927. Above: when they finally stopped imitating Mercédès, Fiat went into the volume-production market in 1913 with their Tipo Zero, a well-built and reasonably-priced two-seater capable of about 50 mph.

closest rivals, and in 1911 a Silver Ghost also did the London–Edinburgh–London trip, returning 24·32 mpg and 78·26 mph. Unkind people said this was making a virtue of necessity, the Rolls-Royce gearchange being notoriously difficult. The gear-changing problem was certainly beginning to attract attention–a good top-gear performance was very much in demand–and in 1911 Vauxhall listed a preselector gearbox as an option. Mercer, who brought out their 5-litre Raceabout the same year (with a guaranteed maximum of 70 mph), produced some cars with magnetic transmission in 1912.

A rather unsuccessful attempt to revive Grand Prix racing in France in 1911 finished up as a second-rate race with a very small entry, and the little 1 327 cc Bugatti which came second to a 10-litre Fiat was, in fact, two laps behind. For the Coupe de *l'Auto*, won by Delage, cars were restricted to 3 litres. In the Austrian Alpine Trial, now more important than the Prince Henry series, even Austro-Daimler turned to smaller cars, but their 2·2-litre shaft-drive model still took the first five places.

The big American race of 1911 was the first Indianapolis 500, held on Memorial Day before a crowd of 80 000 spectators. All the cars in the race except Ray Harroun's winning Marmon Wasp were two-seaters with riding mechanics. When the other drivers protested that Harroun would be unable to see other cars overtaking, he fitted what is thought to be the first rear-view mirror used on any car. That year, too, Ralph Burman exceeded 140 mph at Daytona with the Blitzen Benz.

The big Benzes that scored so many racing successes in America inspired the 15-litre chain-driven cars which Lorraine-Dietrich entered for the revived French GP, a marathon 956-mile event held at Dieppe in 1912. Also chain-driven, the Fiats had 14 137 cc ohc engines, but the Peugeots were much more up to date–fairly light cars with detachable

wire wheels, shaft drive, and very efficient 7·6-litre four-cylinder engines having twin overhead camshafts and four valves per cylinder. Zuccarelli Ernest Henry, Goux and Boillot have all been credited with playing a part in their design. And it was a Peugeot that won at 68·45 mph, Boillot driving, with Wagner's Fiat as runner-up.

Peugeot had built a similar but smaller car for the 1912 Coupe de l'Auto, held concurrently with the Grand Prix and still run to a 3-litre limit. It came as a surprise to all when three Sunbeams, reliable but quite simple cars with side valve engines, occupied the first three places, the fastest of them also finishing third in the Grand Prix. The effect of racing success was shown by the Sunbeam company's balance sheets before and after this race; in 1911 they made a profit of £41 000, in 1913 it rose to £94 909.

There were many other technical advances in 1912. Cadillac became the first motor manufacturer to fit electric lighting and starters as standard, BSA made the first frameless all-steel bodies, Darracq

Peugeot built a team of very advanced twin ohc cars for the 1912 French Grand Prix, a race that totalled no less than 956 miles. The victorious Georges Boillot, here seen refuelling, beat cars with twice the Peugeot's engine capacity.

Two years later, in the last pre-war French Grand Prix, Boillot tried valiantly to prevent a German victory, but the Mercédès team swept through to the first 1-2-3 finish in Grand Prix history, Lautenschlager leading Wagner (seen here at a pit stop) and Salzer.

experimented with a rotary-valve engine, Vauxhall used a multi-plate clutch, and some Charrons were fitted with hydraulic transmission. The dipstick at last made its appearance. William Richard Morris of Oxford designed his first car, a simple but thoroughly sound little two seater which was to provide cheap and reliable transport for the ordinary man in England, as Ford's Model T had already done for his counterpart in America. The Morris Oxford was announced in October, but no car was ready for the Olympia show, and the one exhibited early in 1913 had a wooden engine, known to the factory employees as the 'wooden horse of Cowley'.

During the 1912 Austrian Alpine Trial, Radley's 40/50 Rolls-Royce had been unable to restart on the Katschberg Pass, an occurrence which stung the Derby company into making their last official entry into motor sport when they prepared a team of new cars, with four-speed gearboxes, for the 1913 event. They just failed to win the team prize, but collected a satisfactory number of other trophies in the 1620-mile trial. As an unexpected bonus, Salamanca's Rolls won the Spanish GP the same year. Sheffield-Simplex made an attack on the Rolls-Royce market with their new 30 hp model, and Vauxhall brought out a 4-litre version of their Prince Henry cars. A private customer, Higginson, asked for one with engine enlarged to 4½ litres for use in speed events, and thus the famous 30/98–generally regarded as the first British sports car–was born. A further dozen were built before the outbreak of war. Another lively but very different British machine, a three-wheeler Morgan, won

Special Rolls-Royce: when Radley's three-speed 40/50 model failed to restart on one hill of the 1912 Alpine Trial, Rolls-Royce built a quartet of four-speed cars known as the 'Continental' for the following year. They performed well, and for the 1914 event Radley was provided with another special Rolls-Royce, this 'Alpine Eagle'. He was the only competitor in his class to finish without loss of marks.

the 1913 Cyclecar GP at Amiens, only to be disqualified as a 'motorcycle and sidecar'.

The Indianapolis 500 Miles was won by Goux at 75·9 mph with one of the previous year's Grand Prix Peugeots. It was, indeed, very much Peugeot's year. Boillot won the French GP again with Goux as runner-up, and Chassagne once more secured third place for Sunbeam. It was just the same in the 1913 Coupe de *l'Auto*, held separately this time and over 956 miles to the mere 579 miles of the Grand Prix; Boillot and Goux were first and second with Peugeots, Kenelm Lee Guinness (the man behind KLG sparking plugs) third with a Sunbeam.

Peugeot's many successes did not go unnoticed elsewhere, and Coatalen, the Sunbeam designer, bought one of the 3-litre cars to take back to England with him. When the TT was revived in 1914, Sunbeam, Vauxhall and Humber all had twin-ohc cars on the starting line. But they were insufficiently tested, and only Guinness' winning Sunbeam survived ahead of two sleeve-valve Minervas, a Straker-Squire and another Minerva. Sixth and last came a French DFP driven by the English agent, a man named W.O Bentley. This had an engine of only 2-litres although the capacity limit was 3310 cc, but Bentley had a secret weapon: it was fitted with aluminium pistons.

It seemed that the French had every reason to feel confident of victory in their next Grand Prix, which in 1914 promised to be the greatest race ever held. For the first time a capacity limit had been imposed, of 4½-litres, with a weight limit of 1100 kg. France, Italy, Britain, Germany, Belgium and Switzerland were all represented among the 37 starters. Every car had either one or two overhead camshafts, apart from one sleeve-valve design, and most had four valves per cylinder. Four manufacturers were using four-wheel brakes. Even Mercédès had 'gone modern' and abandoned chain drive, while their four-cylinder engines had two magnetos and 16 sparking plugs. The Lyons-Givors circuit was to be lapped 20 times, making a total of 468 miles.

Arguments about the race have waged ever since it ended. Was it won and lost on tyre trouble, and if one car's tyres wore out faster than others, were they inferior or was the car simply being over-driven? Were the Peugeots the faster cars in the race, or did the Mercédès have something in hand? Were the German cars driven to a pre-arranged plan, directed from the pits, or did their drivers merely seize what opportunities came their way? Whatever the truth of the matter, Sailer's Mercédès led for the first five laps, breaking the circuit record on his fourth, and then

'Without scientific certainty, however, there may be strong conviction, and mine is that a good six-cylinder, whether Rolls-Royce or Napier, runs more smoothly than any four-cylinder car. . . . Tried by the, to me, infallible touchstone of my own spine, a six-cylinder is a very little, but still distinctly, more luxurious than the best four-cylinder car; but this is not to say that there are not a round dozen of four-cylinder cars on the market which make their passengers as comfortable as any man, or even delicate woman, can reasonably wish to be in this world.'

J.E. Vincent, *Through East Anglia in a Motor Car,* **1907**

Special Standard : the Coventry company is seldom associated with luxury cars, but in Edwardian times they were noted for their big six-cylinder models, some with 4-litre engines. Seventy of these cars were sent out to India for the great Delhi Durbar that followed the coronation of King George V, this particular one being used there by the King.

The famous Morgan started life as a cheap three-wheeler in 1910, and made its reputation in that form, but even before the war there were experiments with rather unlikely-looking four-seater models.

Singer showed what a 'baby car' could do when they brought out their 10 hp two-seater in 1912. At £185 it was deservedly popular, and production continued after the war. This example, registration T.8, was owned by the music-hall comedian, Harry Tate.

retired with engine failure. Boillot's Peugeot then took the lead, but Lautenschlager moved up to harry him unmercifully. Do what he might, the Frenchman could not shake him off; moreover, he had to make eight stops to change tyres, the German only four. On the 18th lap, Lautenschlager swept past into the lead. On the last lap Boillot, in tears, it is said, coasted to a halt with a ruined engine–and Mercédès triumphantly scored the first 1-2-3 victory in the history of Grand Prix racing.

One month later the two nations which had been the leading protagonists in this drama were at war, and it is impossible to avoid looking back on the 1914 French Grand Prix as a sort of dress rehearsal for the sterner struggle that was to follow. The skills that men had learned in developing the motor-car were put to other uses, in the design and manufacture of munitions, tanks and aircraft to wage the world's first mechanised war. Poor Georges Boillot suffered his final defeat at the hands of the Germans, losing his life when his aircraft was shot down over the Western Front in 1916. That same year, car production in America for the first time exceeded the one-million mark, with a grand total of 1 525 578.

PROOF OF THE PUDDING

What were early motor-cars *really* like? We can watch them chuffing by on the Brighton Run, study them in repose in a motor museum, swot up bores and strokes in the reference books–and still have very little idea. You can learn little that is significant about a car from the roadside, or even from the passenger seat, for cars are built to be driven, and only in that way can you get the feel of them properly.

Never having driven a car built earlier than the 1920s, I approached the National Motor Museum at Beaulieu, and to my delight they agreed to help me improve my education. Our choice fell on two cars, separated by 10 years: a 1903 de Dion Bouton Model Q and a 1913 'Prince Henry' Vauxhall, one of the 4-litre models. The 6 hp de Dion was by far the most popular light car of its day, costing around £200 depending on equipment and bodywork; the sort of thing a very 'with it' young country doctor might have chosen in the early years of the century to transport him around his smallish practice. This choice, rather than a pony and trap, would have earned no little disapproval from his older patients. As for the Vauxhall, it was scarcely in the luxury class either, costing about three times as much as the de Dion, but it was built to extremely high standards and represents astonishingly good value for money. With its competition background it could, today, be called a rally car, or perhaps more appropriately a true Grand Touring model, being entirely suited to that purpose. It reveals the kind of motoring that the somewhat more privileged individual could enjoy in the immediate pre-war period.

In appearance the de Dion is an absolute little charmer: even shorter in the wheelbase than an old-type Austin Seven, its tubular chassis about knee-high, and the seat cushion not much lower than the roof of a Mini. The beautifully-made wooden wheels carry tyres that would look small on a motorbike, and the mudguards curve cheerfully upwards like quizzical eyebrows. Indeed, the shape of every component is a delight, from the elegant brass-inlaid bonnet to the pleated red-leather settee that forms the seat. If it is possible to feel nostalgic about something one has never known, this is nostalgia on wheels.

To handle this little lady meant learning to drive all over again, and even after several days I still had a lot to learn. The morning routine begins by lifting the bonnet and draining the old oil from the crankcase, checking the brass tanks that hold water and oil, and the fuel tank under the seat (the battery, also under the seat and uncomfortably close to the petrol, is a modern large-capacity one and needs no attention). I then give the engine a charge of oil with the hand pump on the driver's side of the dashboard, and open the petrol tap.

The 700 cc single-cylinder engine is mounted vertically under the bonnet, but the big brass carburettor, being gravity-fed, is almost out of sight at the bottom of a long induction pipe (also brass; almost everything is). The next step is to flood the carburettor and turn the engine

Built in thousands, the de Dion 6 hp Model Q certainly earned its type-name of 'La Populaire'.

Le départ de l'Ambusqué

Another delightful René Vincent painting, dated 1915, depicts the hero's departure to the wars—by car, of course, with such essential impedimenta as champagne, a tantalus, coffee pot and grinder.

Above, right: *in 1909 de Dion, long famed for their light and simple cars, made a determined effort to market a luxury model with this 35 hp V-8. Somehow it never really caught on, but Cadillac followed their example in 1914 and later claimed to have originated the V-8 engine.*

Right: *while de Dion were turning to larger models, other French car-makers were disturbed by a sharp increase in motoring taxation and the price of petrol. The result was the world's first cyclecar, the extra-ordinary Bedélia. That the driver sat* behind *the passenger was only one of its peculiarities; the various controls were shared between the two, which must have given rise to some fascinating arguments at times.*

DE DION V8, 1911

over a couple of times, to the accompaniment of burping noises from the atmospheric inlet valve. I then check the setting of the ignition, throttle and gear levers, switch on the ignition, take a proper hold of the starting handle (thumb *beside* fingers) and pull smartly up, keeping a wary eye on the exposed spindle of the water-pump, which is just waiting to wind me into the works if I lean over with a dangling necktie. Usually she starts first time, making a noise like a worn-out concrete mixer and quivering all over like an excited puppy. While she warms up I check the tyre treads for flints or sharp stones; there is no spare, after all, the wheels being non-detachable. If you have a puncture you mend it, there and then.

So now, after about a quarter of an hour, I am ready to go. No goggles, because I wear spectacles, and fortunately it isn't raining, so I only need something warm—and, for preference, old, for to rephrase the proverb in relation to veteran cars, where there's brass there's muck. In the big wooden box behind the seat I have some waterproof sailing togs, spare petrol, tools, and, for a special reason, a brick. Using the very necessary step iron I climb up on to the driving seat, gaze at the controls, and remember what they told me at Beaulieu: 'You need three hands to drive this car.'

Actually I would say five is a bare minimum. There are only two pedals: one engages reverse gear (using the heel) and the other is in effect a decelerator, not an accelerator, because it actuates a transmission brake and also alters the exhaust-valve lift; like all such brakes it is hard on the transmission, and it also tends to stall the engine, so I try not to use it at all.

Everything else is done with the hands. On the right is a long lever which operates contracting band brakes on the rear wheels, and heaven help me if I forget that it has to be *pushed*, not pulled. On the steering column is a lever which, like the brake pedal, reduces the exhaust-valve lift, and on the right is a separate pillar carrying the ignition and throttle levers. I have been told to control my speed with the latter, but a contemporary motor manual says that engine speed should be controlled by ignition timing and exhaust-valve opening, using this 'throttle' to adjust mixture strength. I still don't know. The only thing I'm sure about is that none of these levers seems to exert much effect on the engine, which chunters away with very little regard for my wishes in the matter.

The entire car is still quivering like a pop singer at the microphone, and if my eyes do not deceive me there are at least six brass headlamps on each of the dashboard brackets.

A larger lever on another separate pillar, to the left of the steering column, is the gear lever and clutch combined, for the ingenious de Dion arrangement provides two constant-mesh gears engaged by expanding clutches: back with the lever for 'low', forward for 'high', or ditto plus heel pedal for reverse.

To get under way, then, I release the side brake (right hand), advance the ignition and open the throttle (right hand), gently ease the gear lever back (left hand), and, of course, hold the thick, wood-rimmed steering wheel (left or right hand). Try it some time on a hill, when all these movements have to be made simultaneously, and among other things you'll understand why I carry a brick.

There are three roads out of my village. One has a gradient of about 1 in 7, and when I tried it I came to rest in a cloud of steam just before the top; no room to turn, so I had to reverse for half-a-mile on the side brake. The second road meets, downhill, a fast main highway at a concealed junction—and the de Dion is now worth £6000 or so at the ripe old age of 70. So I take the third road, a narrow one winding through the forest, with patches of unmelted snow in the shadier parts. The ride is surprisingly comfortable apart from a good deal of kick back through the steering, and from the high driving position I can see right over the bare winter hedges; just as well, with de Dion brakes, and a fair chance of encountering a fast-moving modern car on one of the bends.

On low gear I get up to 5 or 6 mph, maybe a little more, then ease the lever into 'high'. The note of the engine changes abruptly from a rapid clatter to a steady thump, and we leap forward at 20 mph or so. For a quick gear change there is little point in closing the throttle because the engine responds so slowly, and now I seem to be absolutely flying along. It is very exhilarating but I begin to feel apprehensive, having found that this de Dion is prone to develop a sudden and alarming steering wobble which is not only unpredictable but also nearly uncontrollable. At the first downhill stretch, therefore, using a tip I read in an old motoring book, I switch off the ignition and go down against compression on a dead engine, which saves the brakes and makes me feel slightly more in control of things.

Every three or four miles I pull the pump handle halfway up, turn the selector to *Moteur*, and give the engine a shot of oil. Very afraid of damaging the engine, I am inclined to overdo this, which usually causes

The driving position of popular cars had changed somewhat in 70 years or so—the 1903 de Dion alongside a Mini.
Bottom: *intended for the same market, the 1904 Elmore from Ohio certainly lacked the grace of the French car. The 'bonnet' was a dummy, for the two-stroke engine was under the floor.*

Beaulieu's de Dion has great charm, with its cheerful green bodywork and pleated red leather seat. Mechanically, it is ingenious rather than impressive.

an oiled-up plug (spare plugs and a spanner have a permanent place in one of the side pockets). On first encountering a hill to be climbed, I take a run at it and change into 'low' well before the engine begins to labour. But there is such an enormous gap between the two ratios that changing down brings me almost to a standstill, and this method of attack, normal for vintage cars, doesn't seem to work very well for veterans. Sometimes I slow right down beforehand, change down, and make my way noisily and laboriously up at little more than a walking pace. Sometimes it seems better (though I don't like doing it) to stay in high gear, ease the ignition back a little, and let the engine slog; my passenger, if any, stands on the step ready to abandon ship if necessary. At the end of a week I am still not satisfied with my hill climbing technique. There is obviously quite a knack to it, and sometimes I can get up one particular hill, sometimes I can't.

When I first arranged to borrow the de Dion I had great plans to visit various friends, take it through town traffic, and range far and wide about the surrounding countryside. These notions suffered a drastic change after I had actually driven the car. Using the local one-inch map and paying careful attention to contour lines, I picked out a circular route of 17 miles that avoided all heavy traffic and steep hills. Even this, however, included a 3-mile stretch of almost straight, featureless road climbing very gradually up a windswept valley, and to cover that section seemed to take forever. As a lifelong motoring enthusiast I hate to admit it, but nothing could have been more boring than sitting on a clattering piece of machinery, perishing cold despite many layers of clothing, while it trundled along this apparently endless road at a steady 15 mph or so. Fortunately the road passed the 'White Horse', which we seldom did, and there (the de Dion being a French car) we could contemplate the sublime logic of referring to brandy as *eau-de-vie*.

The Prince Henry Vauxhall of 10 years later is very much a motor-car, of most imposing size and appearance. And it goes just as well as it looks.

Early motor-cars, their opponents kept saying, were noisy and smelly. Judging by the de Dion, they were right. In high gear the noise was not too obtrusive, in low gear it was very much worse, and when the car was stationary, the engine running light, it was appalling. The carburation was so poor that it really did stink, sitting there in a thickening cloud of unburnt hydrocarbons. And the vibration was unbelievable—no wonder the lamps were wired to their brackets, and on one occasion the side brake, though firmly applied, vibrated clean out of its ratchet. Every day as I hosed the car down (for it got very dirty even on a short run) I would do a quick check-over, and as often as not found something working loose. In 1903, when roads were dusty and rough, maintenance must have been almost a full-time job.

In due course the de Dion went back to Beaulieu on its trailer, and a couple of weeks later I went to collect the Prince Henry Vauxhall. 'You won't need a trailer for *this!*' said the curator, Michael Ware, and how right he was.

Just as well, too. The Vauxhall is a big car, slightly over 10 feet in the wheelbase compared with the de Dion's 6 feet-plus, and so well proportioned that there is nothing of the 'early perpendicular' about it although the driving position is still very high: the Vauxhall seat-cushion is 36 inches from the ground, the de Dion's 41 inches. The bodywork has a unity, a freedom from 'bittiness', that the earlier car completely lacks, suggesting that it has been conceived as a whole rather than being arrived at by accident. An immensely handsome vee radiator dictates the shape of the bare aluminium bonnet (with two flutes which on this model's direct descendant, the famous 30/98, are carried back to the scuttle), and the bonnet line runs unbroken to the cockpit without a trace of the ugly bulge that, on many contemporary cars, still revealed the transition from bare dashboard to 'scuttle dash' to flush-sided bodywork.

At a slightly lower level than the scuttle, reached by a graceful curve, the horizontal line continues right to the back of the car, but with a stroke of sheer genius, the back of the front seat is slightly raised and merged with the side panels to provide a subtle reminder of the earlier 'Roi des Belges' coachwork in all its glory. The mudguards have the same unity, linked by the running boards to sweep in one line the full length of the car.

The tyres are a slightly fatter version of the beaded-edge pneumatics on the de Dion, but fitted to centre-lock wire-spoked wheels of the familiar Rudge-Whitworth type. The CAV electric headlamps, nickel plated and carried in fork mountings, are $10\frac{1}{2}$ inches in diameter. The windscreen, unframed along its top edge and fixed by 'fold-flat' brackets to a piece of varnished mahogany on the scuttle, looks rather an after-thought, and offers one of the few reminders that this car is 60 years old. In general, however, the appearance of the Prince Henry would still have been completely acceptable to most people 20 years after it was built. To me, and to many others, it is still joyously acceptable today.

Technically there is nothing in the least complicated about it: channel-steel chassis, semi-elliptic leaf springs front and rear, steering by worm-and-sector box. The engine, catalogued as 25 hp, is a robust four-cylinder side valve unit of 4-litre capacity, one litre more than those actually used in the Prince Henry Trials a few years before. Exposed flywheel, Hele-Shaw multiple-disc clutch, separate four-speed gearbox, and shaft drive to live rear axle. Ignition is by magneto, but there is a battery in a mahogany box on the offside running board, the starter motor is obviously a later addition, and somewhere there is a dynamo (I never did find it, but the ammeter showed a charge . . .). The up-in-the-air steering wheel, 17 inches in diameter, is surmounted by a nickel plated ring with ignition lever and hand throttle, plus a smaller lever for mixture control.

Although involved in motor racing since their steam days, de Dion later dropped out of the sport for a time, apart from occasional works entries. But they did make a 1 260 cc single-cylinder 'Type de Course' model, with which Count Taska came 3rd in the 1908 Palermo Cup Race.

The first step in starting is to turn on the petrol and pump up about a pound of pressure in the tank, using a small hand pump inside the cockpit (once the engine has started, an automatic pump holds the pressure at twice that level). Then you flood the big White and Poppe carburettor, set the controls, switch on and press the starter. A subterranean rumble and, after a little time, the big engine starts with a deep and throaty note from the exhaust.

The hand brake is outside, on the right, and the gate-change gear lever is also on the right, just inside the body, so there is no door on that side; you use the tradesmen's entrance or hop over (and it is a big hop, the cockpit side being chest-high to a six-footer). Clutch pedal on the left, transmission brake on the right, throttle pedal in the middle. The Beaulieu staff gave me a cheery wave and left me to my own devices with what I am assured is close on £20000-worth of motor-car; I didn't even have a trial run in the grounds before taking it away.

But I found the Prince Henry simplicity itself after the de Dion, even though I'd never used a right-hand gear change and the gate is the 'wrong' way round (third and top on left, first and second on right), even though I'd been particularly asked not to use the transmission brake, so that all braking had to be done on the side-lever. Normally I adjust fairly slowly to an unfamiliar car, but there is something about this machine that inspires immediate confidence, and within the first 10 miles I was paced by another car (there is no speedometer) at a little over 70 mph. It takes a measure of assurance to do that, even on a clear road, with no front brakes at all.

Initial getaway is a little slow, but (making use of the ignition control) the middle-range acceleration is surprising–surprising, that is, until you discover that this big car has 75 bhp under the bonnet and weighs only 26 cwt. The high top gear gives a glorious seven-league-boots impression and you feel that the engine is utterly unbreakable, encouraged by a steady 15/20 psi reading on the oil-pressure gauge. You bowl along in splendid style with a high-pitched whistle from the carburettor, a low boom from the exhaust.

On all but the worst surfaces the ride is good. There is something magnificently balanced about the suspension which makes the Prince Henry, on its narrow-section tyres inflated to about 50 psi, one of the most sure-footed cars I have ever driven; I simply didn't notice, until somebody else pointed it out, that there were no front shock absorbers at all! So far from having difficulty in keeping up with modern traffic, you frequently overtake other cars, the gear change dropping cleanly into third with absolute precision.

Snags? Few that I could see. The right hand gets a bit busy at times, for it is used both to slow down and to change gear, but when the Prince Henry was new its owner would not have been afraid of damaging the transmission by making full use of the footbrake, and would therefore have had fewer howling draughts up his sleeve. Obviously it is better, as car designers realised some ten years later, to have brakes on all four wheels operated by the foot, not the hand. It would be nice to have a speedometer, a fuel gauge and a windscreen wiper. No doubt the headlamps (temporarily out of action) would scarcely measure up to the car's performance after dark. But these things are of minor importance compared with the fact that the Prince Henry Vauxhall is a joy to drive, a joy to look at.

Having tried both, I would feel no great urge to borrow the de Dion again or to drive it more than 20 miles or so at a time. At the drop of a hat I would take the Vauxhall from here to Monte Carlo, and count myself a fortunate man to do so. That, to my mind, is a measure of the difference between these two cars: one of 1903, the other of 1913.

INDEX